Praise for *Successful Single-Sex Classrooms*

"Given that this is the first book of its kind and that the popularity of single-gender classrooms is rapidly growing across the country I feel it is essential that not only my district, but all districts that are offering single-gender classrooms buy this book for their staff."

— *Dave Curtis, 5th grade teacher (all boys), Kenowa Hills Public Schools, MI*

"I would certainly recommend this book to practicing professionals seeking to implement single-sex schools and classes. As a researcher, I meet many people seeking practical answers for their how-to questions. One of my primary recommendations as a researcher is that teacher-training and professional development support must be provided when schools implement single-sex classes. This book provides a resource that supports that recommendation. Both the language and arrangement of the book make the content appropriate for teachers and administrators who seek to implement single-sex classes."

— *Frances Spielhagen, assistant professor, Education Division, Mount Saint Mary College, Newburgh, NY*

"This book is a well-timed resource for educators who are expressing interest in single-sex schooling in the United States. Questions about strategies, techniques, curriculum, and the legality of single-sex schooling are on the rise as districts, schools, administrators, educators, and parents are considering single-sex classes as a program choice for students. Moreover, administrators are in need of guidance with respect to planning, implementing, assessing, communicating, and maintaining single-sex programs. This book achieves high marks as a practical and useful manual to guide teachers as they work in single- or mixed-gender classrooms."

— *Doug MacIsaac, Nina B. Hollis Institute for Educational Reform, professional development school coordinator, Stetson University, DeLand, FL*

Previous Books by Michael Gurian and Kathy Stevens

The Minds of Boys: Saving Our Sons from Falling Behind in School and Life

Strategies for Teaching Boys & Girls—Elementary Level (with Kelley King)

Strategies for Teaching Boys & Girls—Secondary Level (with Kelley King)

Previous Books by Michael Gurian

Parenting

Nurture the Nature

The Wonder of Children (previously published as *The Soul of the Child*)

The Wonder of Girls

The Wonder of Boys

A Fine Young Man

The Good Son

What Stories Does My Son Need? (with Terry Trueman)

Psychology

What Could He Be Thinking?

Love's Journey

Mothers, Sons and Lovers

The Prince and the King

Boys and Girls Learn Differently!: A Guide for Teachers and Parents
(with Patricia Henley and Terry Trueman)

The Boys and Girls Learn Differently Action Guide for Teachers
(with Arlette C. Ballew)

Business

Leadership and the Sexes: Using Gender Science to Create Success in Business
(with Barbara Annis)

For Young Adults

Understanding Guys

From Boys to Men

Fiction and Poetry

The Miracle

An American Mystic

The Odyssey of Telemachus

Emptying

As the Swans Gather

Successful Single-Sex Classrooms

A PRACTICAL GUIDE TO TEACHING BOYS AND GIRLS SEPARATELY

Michael Gurian
Kathy Stevens
Peggy Daniels

JOSSEY-BASS
A Wiley Imprint
www.josseybass.com

Published by Jossey-Bass
A Wiley Imprint
989 Market Street, San Francisco, CA 94103-1741—www.josseybass.com

Jossey-Bass books and products are available through most bookstores. To contact Jossey-Bass directly call our Customer Care Department within the U.S. at 800-956-7739, outside the U.S. at 317-572-3986, or fax 317-572-4002.

Jossey-Bass also publishes its books in a variety of electronic formats. Some content that appears in print may not be available in electronic books.

Library of Congress Cataloging-in-Publication Data

Gurian, Michael.
  Successful single-sex classrooms : a practical guide to teaching boys and girls separately / Michael Gurian,
    Kathy Stevens, Peggy Daniels.
      p. cm.
  Includes bibliographical references.
  ISBN 978–0–7879–9732–8 (pbk.)
  1. Single-sex schools—United States. 2. Single-sex classes (Education)—United States. I. Stevens,
Kathy, 1949– II. Daniels, Peggy. III. Title.
  LB3067.4.G87 2009
  371.82—dc22

                                                                                          2008045994

Printed in the United States of America
FIRST EDITION

PB Printing   10 9 8 7 6 5 4 3 2 1

ABOUT THIS BOOK

Successful Single-Sex Classrooms: A Practical Guide to Teaching Boys and Girls Separately is an invaluable resource for teachers working with students in single-sex environments. It weaves together brain science and classroom strategies in a way that is both easily understandable and immediately applicable. This is the kind of book that teachers want—one that combines the right balance of "just enough" theory to help teachers become knowledgeable and a "whole bunch" of practice so that they can jump right in with the strategies on Monday morning.

We've organized this book around several important strategy domains so that you can go right to the sections you need. If you are thinking about a single-sex program in your school or community, Chapter One will give you success data from other programs around the country. You can use this data to help you make your case for single-sex options. In Chapter Two, you'll find a great deal of information on how the brains of boys and girls learn differently. The remaining chapters provide strategies that have proven successful in classrooms.

As you read the chapters, you'll find strategies for everything from relationship building to core curricula teaching. Language arts, math, science, social studies, and much more are covered, and strategies are applied directly to teaching boys and teaching girls. We hope you'll appreciate the comments from teachers outlining how they've innovated and used these strategies, and also from students about their own learning in boys-only and girls-only classes.

A highlight of this book is that many of the strategies used for teaching one subject can work for others. You can apply the extensive classroom activities and ideas across all content areas. We wanted to create a book for teachers that can be read and reread many times over and that is a source of creativity and inspiration for years to come. We hope that our ideas may infuse a new level of excitement for you in your work with girls and boys, and greater learning for all the students in your classroom.

THE AUTHORS

Michael Gurian is a social philosopher, family therapist, corporate consultant, and the *New York Times* bestselling author of twenty-five books published in twenty-one languages. The Gurian Institute, which he cofounded, conducts research internationally, launches pilot programs, and trains professionals.

As a social philosopher, Michael has pioneered efforts to bring neurobiology and brain research into homes, workplaces, schools, and public policy. A number of his groundbreaking books in child development, including *The Wonder of Boys, Boys and Girls Learn Differently!, The Wonder of Girls,* and *What Could He Be Thinking?,* as well as *The Minds of Boys* (coauthored with Kathy Stevens), have sparked national debate. His newest work, *Nurture the Nature* (2007), provides a revolutionary new framework, based in neurobiology, by which to understand and care for children all the way from birth to adulthood.

A former university instructor, Michael has worked as a consultant to school districts, families, therapists, community agencies, and other organizations. He keynotes regularly at conferences and has lectured at such leading institutions as Harvard University, Johns Hopkins University, Stanford University, and UCLA. His training videos are used by Big Brother and Big Sister agencies throughout North America.

Michael's work has been featured in various media, including the *New York Times,* the *Washington Post, USA Today, Newsweek, Time, Educational Leadership, Parenting, Good Housekeeping, Redbook,* and on the *Today Show, Good Morning America,* CNN, PBS, and National Public Radio.

Kathy Stevens, executive director of the Gurian Institute, is an international presenter and coauthor of *The Minds of Boys*. Her work has been featured in national publications including *Newsweek, Reader's Digest, Educational Leadership, Education Week, National School Board Journal,* and *Library Journal.*

Kathy has over twenty-five years of experience working in the nonprofit sector, focusing on children, youth, families, and women's issues. Her professional experience includes teaching music in Pre-K–8, designing and administering programs in early childhood care and education, domestic violence, juvenile corrections, adult community corrections, teen pregnancy prevention, cultural competency, and women's issues. Much of her early work was done in economically disadvantaged minority communities.

In addition to her work with the Gurian Institute, Kathy has designed and delivered training for the Federal Bureau of Prisons, Virginia Department of Corrections, Girl Scouts, U.S. Navy Ombudsman Program, Disproportionate Minority Confinement Task Force, and a variety of nonprofit organizations. As a diversity trainer, she was honored to participate in the Children's Defense Fund's Institute for Cultural Competency at the former Alex Haley Farm in Tennessee.

Kathy lives in Colorado Springs with her husband. She has two sons and seven grandchildren.

Peggy Daniels, certified trainer for the Gurian Institute, has been a classroom teacher in both public and independent schools and a school administrator for most of the last thirty-four years. She has a Master's Degree in School Administration from Western Carolina University and currently serves as Middle School Principal at Carolina Day School in Asheville, North Carolina. In recent years, her personal professional development has focused on the study of gender-based brain differences and nature-based strategies for teaching and learning.

Six years ago, Peggy initiated the adoption of single-sex instruction for teaching the core curriculum in sixth and seventh grades at Carolina Day. Under her leadership, the single-sex program has been a great success, and teachers throughout the school (grades Pre-K–12) receive ongoing training and support from the Gurian Institute to incorporate best practices across the grades for teaching boys and girls differently. Three years ago Carolina Day was designated a Gurian Institute Model School for its commitment to understand the minds of boys and girls and for working to meet their educational needs.

Peggy enjoys teaching parents, teachers, and administrators strategies for brain-compatible learning. As an Institute trainer, she leads workshops and professional development opportunities for schools across the nation, including presentations for community and professional organizations.

Peggy and her husband, Rick, reside in Asheville, North Carolina. They have two grown children, Sam and Rachel.

ABOUT THE GURIAN INSTITUTE

If you would like to help your school and community better understand how gender affects learning and living, please contact the Gurian Institute. Through our four divisions—Education, Family, Human Services, and Corporate—we provide training and services to schools, school districts, institutions of higher education, parent groups, businesses, youth organizations, juvenile and adult correctional institutions, medical and mental health professionals, religious organizations, and others serving boys and girls, and men and women.

We also provide keynotes and breakouts at conferences worldwide. There are Gurian Institute trainers throughout the United States, and in Canada, Australia, China, France, and Korea.

We are committed to helping school districts, corporations, and agencies become self-sufficient through internal training-of-trainer models. These are ongoing and serve populations over the long term.

A highlight of our training year is our annual Summer Training Institute in Colorado Springs. Professionals join together for four days of training and networking. Some individuals become certified on the fifth day.

The Institute also provides books, workbooks, training videos for educators and parents, newsletters for parents and teachers, online courses and live chats, as well as other products.

For more information on services, products, and our philosophy, please visit www.gurianinstitute.com.

ACKNOWLEDGMENTS

We at the Gurian Institute have been invited into classrooms around the country, meeting wonderful educators who have honored us by allowing us to help them expand their toolbox. This book could not have been written without teachers sharing their successes and students adding their voices. We are grateful to each and every one of them. Our special thanks go to:

- Our Gurian Institute Certified Trainers, most of whom are educators just like you—principals, classroom teachers, curriculum specialists, school counselors—working in schools rich in diversity, challenge, and success.

- The outstanding educators in the Gurian Institute Model Schools, and all the schools that have honored us by inviting us into their classrooms and that willingly shared their experiences working with single-sex initiatives.

- Lynn Ritvo, Doug MacIsaac, Dave Curtis, and all the professionals who took time in their already overbooked lives to review the manuscript and offer invaluable feedback.

- Dr. Frances Spielhagen of Mount Saint Mary College in Newburgh, New York, whose dedication to quality research in the field of single-sex education and consultation proved invaluable as we worked on this book.

The editorial staff at Jossey-Bass is simply the best in the business! The wisdom and support of Lesley Iura, Julia Parmer, Margie McAneny, Dimi Berkner, Pamela Berkman, Justin Frahm, and, as always, Alan Rinzler, have combined to make this truly a better book than it would have been without their help.

For Gail, Gabrielle, and Davita
— Michael

Thanks Michael, for once again giving me the opportunity to be part of something truly amazing. And to all the teachers and students who were willing to share their stories. And to Don, for always making the coffee!
— Kathy

My sincere appreciation to Michael and Kathy for involving me in this project. I could not have done my part without the support, patience, and understanding of my family, especially my husband, Rick. This book is the work of many—students, parents, and educators across the United States. Thanks to all who contributed valuable information, strategies, and boy- and girl-friendly activities. And special thanks to my colleagues and the students of Carolina Day.
— Peggy

CONTENTS

PART ONE

The Case for Single-Sex Classrooms

Research shows that some students may learn better in single-sex environments. . . . Every child should receive a high quality education in America and every school and district deserves the tools to provide it.

—Margaret Spellings, U.S. Secretary of Education

The idea behind providing choices in public schools is, for me, one of the best ways that we can ensure choices of learning environments that will maximize the achievements of every student. I think we need to be creative and think outside the box.

—Hillary Clinton, U.S. Senator

Single-Sex Classrooms Are Succeeding

Educators at single-sex schools already get it: equality is the goal, and there may be more than one path to the destination.

—Karen Stabiner, journalist and author

If you are reading this book, you probably fall into one of several categories. You may be a teacher or school administrator who is considering the possibility of implementing single-sex classes in your school; you may already work in a school that has incorporated single-sex instruction, and you are seeking more knowledge and information to make your program successful; or you may be a teacher, parent, or policy maker wondering just how successful single-sex classroom instruction is proving to be, and why.

Over the last decade, the Gurian Institute has trained over forty thousand teachers in more than two thousand schools and districts, both coed and single-sex. Our trainers have worked with public and private schools, Montessori schools, and a variety of charter and independent schools in fifteen countries; we have therefore been able to see what is working and not working around the globe. In this chapter, we will feature some of the schools and communities that have utilized our resources to help set up and maintain their successful single-sex programs.

The resurgence of single-sex instruction is one of the most powerful educational innovations of the last decade (also one with a long history across the globe). People who advocate for single-sex instruction do not generally claim it to be the only successful way to teach boys and girls, and they are very clear on its mission: gender equality. As they employ this innovation, they often find that it can be an effective way to teach many boys and girls in certain subjects, in certain communities, and that it is especially effective as a response to the ongoing cultural need to discover measurable and substantial achievement gains for both genders.

"I teach both coed and single-sex classes. I like them both in their own ways. They are each unique. They each bring different things out of the students and out of me. I'm glad my school gives the option of single-sex classes. Some kids are flourishing in those classes who were losing their way when they got preoccupied with the other gender."

—Layne, middle school teacher, New Jersey

A SHORT HISTORY OF THE "NEW" SINGLE-SEX OPTION

Broad-based single-sex programs have been available in independent schools, unrestricted by federal regulation, for centuries. From those schools, many with long-established programs, a number of single-sex instructional models have been maintained, many using the same instructional strategies for years. Day schools have offered single-sex classes schoolwide, or in particular divisions (usually lower or middle school), or only in specific grades. Some boarding schools serve only boys or girls; others may serve both boys and girls, but in separate facilities.

Prior to 2006, single-sex classes in public schools were generally limited to physical education and sex education classes, but a growing gender gap in performance and achievement has led public schools to reexamine single-sex possibilities. As public schools looked at piloting single-sex classes, legal challenges arose. Schools and districts, such as Southside Junior High School in Denham Springs, Louisiana, were taken to court. With the support of the ACLU, a parent legally challenged Southside's plan to implement single-sex classes in the fall of 2006, delaying the program a year.

In October 2006, the U.S. Department of Education announced changes in Title IX regulations, expanding opportunities for public schools to legally offer the option of single-sex instruction. Within certain parameters set out in the final Title IX single-sex amended regulations, public schools are now allowed to include single-sex classes as a part of their educational program, if they believe those classes will improve student learning and achievement. (Document 34 CFR Part 106, the complete Title IX regulations, is available and may be downloaded directly from the Department of Education Web site: www.ed.gov/index.jhtml.)

Today, in increasing numbers, public and independent schools are investigating the option of single-sex instruction as a means of further supporting and improving the educational growth of boys and girls. This option is proving to be an exciting alternative for improving academic performance and for creating classrooms that are more boy- and girl-friendly.

Helping Boys and Girls Succeed—The Logic of Single-Sex Instruction

At the classroom level, single-sex instruction offers specific gender-friendly opportunities for enhancing learning by directly addressing many of the challenges and stressors in boys' and girls' educational and personal lives.

DID YOU KNOW? SINGLE-SEX EDUCATIONAL POSSIBILITIES

The single-sex classroom can often

- Allow for nontraditional teaching techniques and structures that are well suited to aspects of male-female learning differences
- Allow for classes in which the learners are more similar to one another in their stages of physical, mental, and emotional development
- Eliminate certain distractions from the classroom (such as boy-girl flirtation, sexual tensions, gender-based competition), thus increasing concentration and focus
- Allow girls not to worry about making comments in the classroom that boys will ridicule (and vice versa), so that self-esteem can be driven more by performance and less by what members of the opposite sex think and say
- Encourage girls to openly discuss personal issues with which they may be struggling, thus facilitating an earlier, more successful handling of those issues
- Create a comfortable environment for learning, in which girls don't feel the need to worry about how they look or what they wear, and boys feel greater freedom to "be themselves" without posturing and playing to girls' attentions
- Help boys learn self-management through working together, helping each other, and finding safety in being in classes with others who instinctively understand them
- Allow for candid conversations in the classroom (where girls and boys can ask questions and discuss topics they might avoid in a coed setting), thereby creating unique teachable moments for character, leadership, goal setting, girl talk, and boy talk
- Increase boys' willingness to try new things—especially in the arts (performing skits, sharing poetry, and so on)—that they might not be as willing to try in front of girls
- Allow girls to receive more attention, explore broader interests, increase self-confidence and participation, and renew interest in more spatially oriented subjects such as math, science, and technology

- Provide a greater opportunity to help boys with literacy by including more boy-friendly materials
- Enable teachers to create experiences that specifically support boys and girls through creative, gender-specific instructional practices

Single-sex programs, whatever their scope or size in a school, have pursued these potential outcomes and collected success data. Some of the schools and teachers who have utilized Gurian Institute resources and training in *Boys and Girls Learn Differently* have shared their success data with us so that we could share it with you as you consider the single-sex option, make your case for the option in your community, or continue to maintain your already vital program.

DIFFERENT APPROACHES AND SUCCESS DATA FROM A VARIETY OF SCHOOLS

No two school districts or schools are the same, thus there are many approaches to the creation of single-sex environments in schools. Some districts choose to start single-sex academies; some public schools decide to implement single-sex programs only in their core classes; some private schools are already single-sex or, if coed, decide to implement single-sex classes in certain grades.

Here are examples of success in these different modalities. You can view other schools and districts that have had success in different single-sex modalities on www.gurianinstitute.com/Success, or on the National Association for Single-Sex Public Education (NASSPE) Web site, www.singlesexschools.org.

A Public School District in Atlanta: Two Single-Sex Academies

After several years of planning, the Atlanta Public Schools transformed a struggling middle school into two single-sex academies. The B.E.S.T. Academy at Benjamin Carson, the boys' school, and the Coretta Scott King Young Women's Leadership Academy both opened on separate campuses in the fall of 2007, initially serving sixth graders with a plan to expand through twelfth grade. The B.E.S.T. Academy was championed by Robert Haley, at the time president of The 100 Black Men of Atlanta, which committed support and mentoring for the school, its students, and their families. Five Atlanta chapters of The Links, Incorporated (one of the oldest and largest volunteer service organizations of women who are committed to enriching, sustaining, and ensuring the culture and economic survival of African Americans and other persons of African ancestry) partnered with the girls' school, providing similar support. Both organizations provided substantial assistance, including purchasing uniforms for the charter class of 2007–2008. Many other community organizations also partnered with the Atlanta Public Schools to support this initiative.

The staff of the boys' school focused on closing the achievement gap in literacy, recognizing that reading skills would affect every content area for their students from sixth grade through high school graduation and into college. Implementing best-practice single-sex strategies that have proven to help boys succeed, the teachers and administrators at the boys' school are excited about the strides their students have already made and will make in the future.

The staff of the girls' school focused on increasing the girls' use of technology. The teachers used Promethean Boards in the areas of math and science, overhead projectors, thin client computers, digital cameras, iPods for podcasting, and LCD projectors. In addition, students created PowerPoint presentations and podcasts for social studies units and concept-based units. On a daily basis, students gathered in the media center, doing research for an event, a project, or a debate.

The struggling students have used the Internet daily to participate in the Achieve 3000 program, a content-based reading program. Principal Melody Morgan said, "I boast that several of the students entered the program as non-readers and have made significant gains this year. We projected gains of 25 percent in this program, and the students actually had an achievement gain of 74.2 percent. They are proud!"

The use of technology is crucial in the global market; encouraging girls' engagement in technology will prepare them to be part of the future economy. A single-sex environment can greatly increase girls' desired participation.

As the schools enter their second year and expand to grades 6 and 7, there are many lessons learned that will help make the second year an ever greater success.

A Statewide Initiative: South Carolina

The South Carolina Department of Education was the first to create a state-level position to lead a statewide single-sex initiative. In July 2007, David Chadwell was appointed director of single-gender initiatives. David is responsible for facilitating the development of single-sex programs across South Carolina, including training teachers; advising program creation; facilitating implementation;  hosting informational sessions for faculty, parents, and community members; and maintaining a network of people interested in or already working in single-gender education.

As of April 2008, there were 97 schools in South Carolina offering some form of single-sex programs across the age levels, with another 214 schools exploring single-sex options. Seventy school districts and nearly 30 percent of the schools in South Carolina are involved in the program, the highest percentage (59 percent) being in middle schools.

Researchers nationwide are watching South Carolina's initiative; this is a great opportunity to learn about the success of single-sex programs as the schools collect and evaluate their data.

A Public, Coed Elementary School: Woodward Avenue Elementary

In 2003 Jo Anne Rodkey, now-retired principal of Woodward Avenue Elementary School in DeLand, Florida, began an opt-in experiment in single-sex instruction, primarily because the boys in her school were lagging significantly behind the girls in reading. The boys were also, by far, the predominant sex in the school's special education classes.

Jo Anne began the process by training her teachers, sending them to related professional development workshops and conferences, and supplying them with the latest research on gender learning differences. They started the program in their kindergarten, second, and fourth grades. As an opt-in program, teachers were able to volunteer to teach in the single-sex classes. To be selected, they had to agree to be purposeful as they planned for instruction, making sure they were using practices suggested from research on brain and gender learning differences. Parents could also choose the program for their children, but it was a guided choice, as Jo Anne wanted to maintain a heterogeneous balance in the classroom in terms of race and academic ability.

Woodward now has optional single-sex classes in grades K–5. The program is successful: individual student gains are noticeable for both boys' and girls' single-sex classes, and both groups do as well or better than the school's regular coed classes. Academic progress being made by the boys includes learning the fundamentals, the basic skills, to help them become good readers. Jo Anne adds that although improving discipline was not a reason Woodward chose to implement their program, she saw fewer problems, especially with boys-only groups. There were fewer office referrals, and she credited this to the fact that the boys' teachers were able to be much more tolerant of boy energy and boy behavior without girls in the classroom.

A Public Middle School: Roosevelt Middle School

Roosevelt Middle School in Oklahoma City, Oklahoma, serves nine hundred students in grades 6–8. One hundred percent of Roosevelt's students qualify for free lunch and 75 percent are minority. In 2005, Roosevelt had a gender gap of 17 percent in reading achievement; 72 percent of Roosevelt's eighth-grade girls scored satisfactory on their state assessment tests, but only 55 percent of eighth-grade boys scored satisfactory.

Principal Marilyn Vrooman began looking for alternatives that would correct this problem. After researching single-sex options, she determined this strategy should be given serious consideration. The teachers agreed, the parents agreed, and after appropriate professional development for all teachers, Roosevelt separated the boys and girls in language arts, math, and technology education.

At the end of the 2005–2006 school year, Roosevelt's boys scored 71 percent satisfactory on the reading CRT and the girls scored 80 percent, narrowing the achievement gap to 9 percent in one year. The 2006–2007 school year was the first year Roosevelt had been off the state's "at risk" list in four years.

A Public Middle School: Wolfe Middle School

Wolfe Middle School in the Center Line School District in Center Line, Michigan, implemented single-sex core courses for sixth graders in language arts, math, social studies, and science during the 2007–2008 school year. They began by receiving training in how boys and girls learn differently (this is the subject of the next chapter in this workbook, and is a crucial starting place for any efforts to close gender and achievement gaps). After one year of single-sex classes, they determined that the significant improvements of both boys and girls in language arts and social studies justified a continuation of single-sex classes in those content areas for 2008–2009. They further decided to move sixth-grade single-sex teachers with their students for seventh grade, a practice known as "looping."

A Public High School: Hope High School

Hope High School in Hope, Arkansas, is a school of approximately eight hundred students in grades 9–12. Assistant Principal Renee Parker works specifically with the ninth and tenth grades, and she saw her ninth-grade students, especially the males, struggling with the transition to high school—failing course after course, and spending numerous days in the detention room for immature behaviors that disrupted classes.

Hope operates on a straight 4 × 4 block schedule where all students have four courses per semester that are ninety minutes long. At the end of the semester, students change to a new set of four courses and have the potential of earning eight credits per year.

In January 2006 Parker looked at her data and found that 12 percent of students in the ninth grade, primarily males, had failed all four courses for the fall semester. These students had placed themselves in serious jeopardy of not graduating with their class, and Parker knew that there had to be some way of making this transition from junior high to high school more successful.

Parker and her colleagues researched gender and learning and obtained professional development for all faculty and staff. Hope High School piloted single-sex classes in the ninth grade in 2006. In January 2007, when the data on student achievement was next gathered, there were no ninth-grade students who failed all four courses, only two had failed two courses, and only eleven had failed one course. Furthermore, discipline referrals for the ninth graders had decreased by 35 percent from the previous fall and the attendance rate had increased by 15 percent.

A Boys' School: Crespi Carmelite High School

Crespi Carmelite High School in Encino, California, is a nonprofit, Catholic, four-year, college preparatory school for young men. In 2005, looking at their performance data and seeking ways to increase student achievement, Father Paul Henson, Crespi's principal, began a two-year process that greatly enhanced the school's ability to establish and maintain a boy-friendly environment. He designed and implemented a two-year professional development plan that included both on-site training for all faculty and staff and sending designated faculty to intensive summer training, thus developing in-house expertise.

Although Crespi had been focused on teaching boys since its founding in 1959, the school was committed to incorporating the latest research on gender and learning into every classroom in the school. Adding to their already deep knowledge base of how to educate boys in a single-sex environment, Crespi's commitment to training has allowed them to increase performance scores to higher levels than before, and to decrease discipline referrals even further.

Crespi, like many boys' schools, approaches developmental issues from a boy-friendly perspective, and implements schoolwide strategies that constantly enhance students' level of success.

A Coed Independent School: Carolina Day School

Carolina Day School is an independent, college preparatory school serving grades Pre-K–12 in Asheville, North Carolina. In the fall of 2004, Carolina Day engaged in a spirited discussion regarding the possibility of implementing single-sex education in the middle school. School administrators listened carefully to parents, students, and faculty; they reviewed research on the topic; they consulted with experts and practitioners. There were differing opinions of considerable merit and, in the end, the community was convinced that Carolina Day should implement single-sex classes in the sixth grade for the fall of 2004–2005, then expand the program to include sixth and seventh grades in 2005–2006.

Research convinced Carolina Day that the best advantage would come from having this program for their younger middle school students. They continued coed classes for eighth grade to provide "transitional experiences in preparation for the upper school." Dr. Beverly Sgro, Head of School, supported the administration's efforts to provide initial intensive onsite training for teachers in grades 5–8 and follow-up training for all lower and upper school faculty.

The middle school of Carolina Day School implemented single-sex instruction in their core classes for sixth and seventh grades in the fall of 2004. Faculty and administrators have stayed current with their training, which began in the spring of 2004.

The single-sex program has been very successful, producing positive academic results for both gender populations, as well as significantly better dynamics, and less social anxiety.

After four years, the middle school at Carolina Day reports these key outcomes:

- Stronger mentoring relationships
- An environment that promotes greater trust and sense of belonging among students
- Teachers who feel more connected with students and with each other
- A greater understanding of how boys and girls learn differently and an emphasis on providing instruction that supports these differences
- More direct ways to deal with students' social and emotional pressures
- Classroom instruction that provides for more teaching and quality learning experiences
- A new energy that causes teachers to be more creative with their ideas and more reflective with their practice

As these and other schools succeed in providing single-sex instruction, their staff have shared testimonials with us. Following are some powerful testimonials of the kind of immediate shifts in student learning and teacher enjoyment that can occur in single-sex classes.

SUCCESS TESTIMONIALS FROM TEACHERS

During the 2007–2008 school year at Winder-Barrow Middle School, math teacher Michael Lofton piloted a single-sex math class for boys and Erica Boswell piloted a single-sex math class for girls.

Lofton told us,

> Since I have been teaching an all-boy math class this year the experience has been very different from my mixed-gender classes. One of the first things that stand out is the camaraderie of the class. I was quick to recognize this because of my coaching experience. In the beginning we discussed the need for the students to be successful in the math class

this year due to then pass/fail criteria of the state standardized test CRCT (Criterion-Referenced Competency Test). We also discussed the need for the class as a whole to be successful.

To meet our goals, we bonded as a team. Early on the boys started encouraging each other. We created teams among our team and had inner competition with study games and activities. The groups changed often so everyone helped and encouraged each other to work harder and study more. We made a phone list so anyone in the class could call another student if they need any help with homework or studying. We also spent a few days in the computer lab learning how to use our textbook online resources. Students with computers and online access helped others without online ability.

It wasn't long before I noticed that grades and comprehension of skills were on the rise. Parents stopped me at football or basketball games telling me how much their son loved the class and was really trying to do well in math.

One student in Lofton's class shared, "The difference between last year and this is that he doesn't yell at us as much as we got yelled at last year." This student is making B's in Lofton's class after a long year of D's in 2006–2007.

"They feel free to make mistakes, and they feel free not to make mistakes," Boswell said of her female students. "A lot of time girls don't want to look too smart. It's a shame that girls have to feel that way at all, but they do. In here, they can feel free to raise their hand for every single question and no one's going to look at them funny."

Dave Curtis, a fifth-grade teacher at Kenowa Hills Public Schools in Michigan, reports:

We have a grade 5–6 building. Each grade has ten classrooms and last year we turned two of the fifth grades into single-gender classrooms, leaving eight others for coed classes. Those students moved up to sixth grade and as a result of parent and student requests, this year our building has four single-gender classrooms in sixth grade and two in fifth. . . . From the onset we heard comments like, "My son finally likes going to school" or "He finally comes home happy and discusses his day." The same was true for the girls' classrooms and we knew we had provided something desirable for our students and parents.

This letter was sent to Peggy by Blake Smith, a high school counselor, several weeks after her school incorporated single-sex education:

Dear Peggy,

Just wanted you all in the middle school to know that if you could step back from all the action and see/hear what is happening in the middle school this year, there is something incredible taking place. Parents at the upper school parents' night program commented on the fantastic atmosphere in the middle school this year, and upper school teachers have been talking about what a fun loving group of teachers the middle school has. The students who roll through the Nash Athletic Center and pass by my office are energized and obviously loving the year so far. It is like we are on a month-long pep-rally or spirit day.

I think this is a reflection of several things (single-sex classes, single-sex advisory, efforts with differentiation and vertical teaming), but mostly a result of the teachers' creativity and enthusiasm, which has been encouraged and supported by the middle school leadership to a degree that I haven't seen in another school yet. By taking some new chances (especially the single-sex instruction), risking long debates with parents, and asking teachers what they think about policy, planning, and pedagogy, there is a contagious excitement in the air that gets passed down to our students. It's not just me—I am hearing it across divisions—and I'm glad to be a part of it too. I don't know if all of you in the middle school can see it as much because you're in it all day—but I suspect you can sense the great energy happening this year.

"Every day is a new day for me, and I really enjoy going to school. I've become a better teacher because I am not satisfied with doing what I've always done before. I am not one to say, 'What I did last year will work with this group too!' I know that I cannot just 'wing it' with my boys. I need a better arsenal

to pull from to keep my boys engaged, and learning, and I have to be 'on my game' all the time. But it is fun and I am learning so much about boys."

—Tessa Michaelos, Woodward Avenue Elementary teacher

At Woodward Elementary in DeLand, Florida, a wife and husband, Deborah and Jim Roberts, teach together and separately in coed and single-sex classes. In the first year of single-sex classes at Woodward, they cotaught a full inclusion, single-sex class of fourth-grade boys. The class included 40 percent minority students, 23 percent general education students, and 12 percent exceptional education students. It was a challenging group, but by the end of the year the test scores for this group of boys were outstanding. On the Florida Writes test, they had some of the highest scores in the district, even outperforming many girls.

The following year, Deborah and Jim looped with this group to fifth grade, and in the third year of the program, Deborah was asked to teach a group of fifth-grade girls while her husband kept the boys. This, too, worked well for both teachers and students. Deborah said, "The changes in the boys and girls, and the challenges for us as teachers, have been very positive. It would be hard to go back to coed classes for these students."

"It is like a wagon train. The boys are the scouts who go out to begin the adventure. The girls are the pioneers, who want to know about things in advance— 'Just how deep is the river before we cross it?' They want the security of knowing the plan and seeing how the pieces fit into that plan."

—Jim Roberts, Woodward Avenue Elementary teacher

Piri Taborosi, a teacher in New York, shared this story:

In 2002, when a new charter school opened in Syracuse, New York, I was its first principal. During the first three days of school, our fifth-grade numbers stabilized into a group of six girls and twenty-two boys. All of these students were at-risk; many had failed grades before; most of them had behavior problems; with the exception of two or three, all of them were reading significantly below grade level. As I contemplated what to do with this group, I made a decision which the company backed me in.

We had two third-grade rooms and had hired two teachers; unfortunately, we only had a total of twenty-two students. I combined the two classes and assigned a full-time teacher assistant to work with the teacher. The other teacher who had been hired to teach third grade was a male, a military man. He was willing to teach fifth grade. Rather than separating the six girls into two groups, with parental support, I kept the girls together and added a few boys. The other class was totally boys and was taught by the male teacher.

All students were tested at the beginning of the year and near the end of the year. Teacher and principal bonuses and pay raises were tied to student achievement. All of our students did very well in the school, but we were not prepared for the phenomenal growth of the boys who were in the single-sex class. This group was also monitored by a local newspaper reporter, who eventually wrote a five-page article about the boys and their class.

"My son loves his teacher who has great empathy and understanding for boys. She provides more hands-on experiences, opportunities to read boy-friendly books and stories (especially about science-related topics—Atlantis, archeology, and paleontology) and more masculine story writing on topics such as pirates, robots, crime-fighting riddles, etc."

—Elementary school parent

These are just a few of the individual testimonials we are hearing from professionals and parents who are opting to innovate in single-sex instruction. Students themselves also speak up about what they are experiencing. Here are examples from a boy and a girl.

"In science we talk more this year because the boys aren't there. I like it when we (girls) get to talk things out. I understand things better when we can talk and share."

—Sophia, middle school girl

"We are not distracted by girls and we don't feel so self-conscious. If I say something a little 'off,' I don't feel as stupid as I would in front of girls."

—Nathan, middle school boy

SINGLE-SEX CLASSROOMS CAN REALLY WORK!

We hope this chapter has provided you with data and testimonials you can use to gain support for single-sex classes in your school or community. As you make your case for single-sex instruction, you may find that resistance lessens when clear data is shown. Data can be a first major tool of persuasion, as well as a real confidence builder for you as a teacher or parent, as you move through the steps to establish a single-sex program.

The second major tool of persuasion, and a very important confidence builder, is an understanding of how boys and girls learn differently. Teachers in coed classes who gain training in male-female brain differences report that both their boys and girls are learning and performing better. Teachers in single-sex classes generally find themselves better able to focus on the brain-gender spectrum for their specific students, giving both girls and boys more of the brain-friendly environment in which they can thrive.

WRAPPING UP THE MAIN POINTS

- Single-sex schooling has a long history of meeting the learning needs of both boys and girls.

- Boy-friendly and girl-friendly environments can help many boys and girls.
- Schools across age levels are piloting single-sex programs, most often with a focus on improving academic performance.
- Single-sex instruction is an opportunity to maximize the learning styles and needs of the male and female brain.

How Boys and Girls Learn Differently

Neuroscientists have continued to make remarkable discoveries about how the human brain grows, develops, and learns. . . . These research insights have allowed scientists to design educational interventions that are amazingly successful.

—David A. Sousa, *How the Brain Learns*

Since the early 1990s there has been an acceleration in brain research. The technology for learning about the brain is improving, and we are constantly seeing new reports on advances in understanding the human brain. Neuroscientists are now able to use sophisticated functional imaging to observe changes of blood flow within the brain. They have also determined how brain chemicals, known as neurotransmitters, permit or inhibit the movement of electronic signals between neurons. Brain imaging technologies have provided scientists with much more detailed information about how different parts of the brain engage during different activities. Neuroscientists are now able to observe the living brain in action; this is a tremendous tool in the ongoing investigation of how and where learning occurs.

Much of this new research has demonstrated that the brains of boys and men are markedly different—anatomically, hormonally, and functionally—from the brains of girls and women. For example, studies of thirty-eight right-handed subjects (nineteen females and nineteen males) by Drs. Sally and Bennett Shaywitz of Yale University, have shown that

- When males read, mainly the left inferior frontal gyrus lights up.
- When females read, the frontal lobe lights up on both sides of the brain.

In addition, in November 2001, neuroradiologist Dr. Joseph Lurito and several other colleagues conducted brain imaging research at Indiana University School of Medicine and found that

- A majority of males use the left side of their brains for listening.
- A majority of females use both sides to process what they hear.

Thus, during certain critical learning activities such as listening and reading, males and females use notably different areas of their brains. The genders learn differently, and even see and hear differently. These differences are real, and they are corroborated in boys and girls and women and men throughout the world and across cultures. They help explain many of the learning behaviors that we have long observed in the classroom. Boys and girls don't process information the same way, and can benefit from strategies that match their learning styles. Though many boys and girls can take their brain differences into coed classrooms and succeed quite well, some do not. Understanding how boys and girls learn can help you, your school, and your own students make a case for single-sex classrooms where they are needed in your community. This understanding also helps with teaching any boy or girl in any setting.

BRAIN-BASED GENDER DIFFERENCES

This chapter will provide you with an overview of the latest information on how boys and girls learn differently. We hope you'll share this research with parents, and with students who are old enough to understand it. This information can become a base of your intuition as you set up your single-sex classroom and strategize delivery of your curriculum. As we explore this information with you, it is crucial that we all agree that every child is an individual, and that male and female brain differences vary both between boys and girls and among boys and girls. Scientists have discovered over one hundred structural variations between the male and female brain, but these differences do not limit a gender—instead, they inspire innovative teaching techniques for each gender.

Structural Differences Between the Male and the Female Brain

Using *magnetic resonance imaging* (MRI), *positron emission tomography* (PET), and *single photon emission computed tomography* (SPECT) scanning technologies, scientists can look at the living brain in action. The most advanced technologies allow researchers to watch actual blood flow in the brain and see exactly where the brain is working. By viewing brains in this way, it becomes clear that male and female brains frequently engage different cortical areas when completing the same tasks.

Over the past couple of decades, technology has helped researchers focus on some specific areas of structural difference between the male and female brain. Following are some of the most significant differences and their potential impact on your classroom.

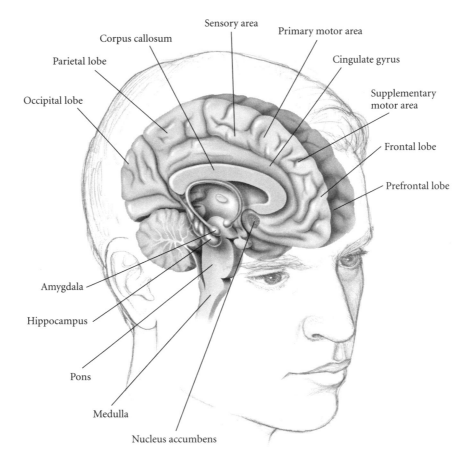

Source: © Copyright Molly Borman-Pullen. Used with permission.

Some Differences in the Male and Female Brain

Part of the Brain	For Girls This Means	For Boys This Means
Cerebral cortex: contains about ten thousand miles of neural connections per square inch; only as thick as about three human hairs; where the serious intellectual functions of the brain (things that need to happen in a classroom) take place—thinking, speaking, remembering, and recalling;	The female brain tends to have more connections between neurons in the cerebral cortex. The increased number and speed of the neural connections may help girls process and respond to classroom information faster, help them make transitions faster, help them	This area matures more slowly in the male brain and may result in boys being more apt to engage in high-risk behavior, respond impulsively and, in general, to "think less before they act."

Part of the Brain	For Girls This Means	For Boys This Means
also facilitates memory functions, voluntary motor behaviors, impulsivity, decision making, planning.	multitask, and help them access needed verbal resources (reading, writing, complex speech) as they engage in learning.	
Frontal cortex: one of the last parts of the brain to mature. It is the CEO of the brain, in charge of executive functions such as planning, organizing, setting priorities, making sound judgments, handling ambiguous information, putting on the brakes by calming unruly emotions.	This area of the brain tends to mature earlier in the female brain, making girls, again, less likely to be impulsive or to engage in risk-taking behavior. Girls are less likely to abuse substances, participate in delinquent behavior, and be involved in accidents. They tend to have lower auto insurance rates as a result.	Again, this area of the brain tends to mature later in males, potentially resulting in boys being more impulsive, more likely to engage in risky behaviors, and more frequently involved in accidents to their bodies and the vehicles they drive! Male insurance rates don't drop until around age twenty-five, when they are more "mature" in general, including having a more mature brain system.
Cerebellum: once believed to be mainly involved in the coordination of our muscles, making us graceful dancers and good athletes. Now we know it is also involved in the coordination of our thinking, our "mental muscles." Physical activity is believed to influence development of the cerebellum.	Healthy brain development, including in the cerebellum, requires physical activity. Today's students are less active overall. Bringing more movement into your curriculum will help girls who are more tolerant of the traditional institutional classroom environment, but who will also benefit from more movement as they develop.	This "doing center" of the brain is larger in the male; coupled with about 15 percent more spinal fluid in the male neural system, this means that messages between the brain and body can move more quickly (and with less impulse control) in the male body. Boys often learn better when their bodies are in motion. Sitting still can frustrate the male system, causing a boy to exhibit behavior that can appear disruptive or impulsive, and that may sometimes land him in the principal's office because he "can't sit still, can't stop touching things, is distracting his classmates," when he's really responding to his biological needs.

(Continued)

Some Differences in the Male and Female Brain *(Continued)*

Part of the Brain	For Girls This Means	For Boys This Means
Corpus callosum: a dense bundle of nerves that connects the two hemispheres of the brain.	In females, this bundle of nerves tends to be denser and larger than in males, resulting in increased cross-talk between the left and right hemispheres. Girls are generally better at multi-tasking, including watching and listening and making notes at the same time. It also may explain why girls tend to tune into their own and others' feelings and move emotional content more quickly into thought and verbal processes. Girls can tell you how they feel as they are feeling it.	With less cross-talk between the hemispheres, the male brain tends to take more time to connect words to actions, or feelings to words. In the classroom this can translate into boys needing more time to process before they can respond to content information, and often needing more time to process before they can explain feelings.
Brain stem: the most primitive part of our brain. Our "fight or flight" response comes from the brain stem, and when we're in crisis this area of our brain takes over.	Girls are less likely to respond physically when challenged, and tend more to use their verbal resources and seek assistance from within their nurturing circle. Girls are generally quicker to ask for help from teachers and parents when they feel threatened.	With their greater levels of spinal fluid connecting the brain and body, boys tend to be poised for "fight or flight" and for a physical response when they feel threatened or emotionally charged. Boys in your class may slam a book, kick a chair, use an expletive, or engage in some other kind of physical display when challenged. This behavior may be the result of an emotionally charged incident when the boy is not given enough time to process the emotional content.
Hippocampus: a key player in converting information from working memory into long-term or permanent memory.	The hippocampus tends to be larger in females and their speed of neural transmissions is faster than in males, resulting in generally increased memory storage for the female brain.	The hippocampus tends to be smaller in the male brain, which may contribute to why males seem to "get over it" more easily than females. Males are less likely to hold grudges. This can

Part of the Brain	For Girls This Means	For Boys This Means
	This can be a source of "drama" between girls, something that could escalate in an all-female setting.	help keep the "drama" to a minimum in the classroom.
Amygdala: a small, almond-shaped structure connected to one end of the hippocampus; plays a very important role in the processing of emotions, especially fear and anger. This is the only part of the brain that is mature at birth.	Girls tend to attach more emotional and sensory detail to events and to remember them longer. They can hold grudges a long time. They often need mentoring in order to see what really is "important" about a situation, and what is overreacting.	The amygdala tends to be larger in males, perhaps contributing to male aggression responses when angry. Researchers believe that the close proximity of the amygdala to the hippocampus suggests that emotional content is "tagged" onto many long-term memories.

Brain Processing Differences Between Boys and Girls

Research has found not only structural differences between the brains of males and females, but variations in how boys and girls use their brains to process information. This has significance for single-sex instruction, as educators develop strategies to implement curriculum that focuses on how to best serve boys and girls.

Here are just a few of the processing differences that have the most impact on learning.

Language Processing Areas   These areas are different in the male and female brain. Males tend to have their language processing areas centralized in the left hemisphere; females tend to have multiple language processing areas in both hemispheres. As a result, females have more access to verbal resources than males and develop language earlier than males.

And this means: Girls tend to have significantly more access to verbal resources when they start school, and throughout life. On average, females use more words than males do (this includes writing and reading). Because of where they are developmentally, it is easier for girls to learn to read and write in kindergarten and first grade. Many boys find these tasks more frustrating at the same age, and though they can perform well once they are developmentally ready, they often

develop negative attitudes about reading and writing as a result of this early period of frustration. Because literacy is the foundation of learning, this difference often results in gender gaps that show up early in elementary school and persist throughout middle and high school.

Spatial Processing Areas   These areas are significantly different in the male and female brain. Testosterone, the primary architect of the male brain, is believed to create more and denser neural connections in the right hemisphere of the male brain, with the result that males have increased resources for spatial reasoning, abstract reasoning, and the like. With less testosterone at work during fetal development, females tend to have less right hemisphere area devoted to spatial resources. Although boys in general test higher in spatial manipulation tests, there is a smaller gender gap in mathematical calculation. Girls tend to be so good at literacy skills that they don't get enough opportunity to practice using their spatial capacities—and when they need them to be sharp, they're not as ready to engage.

And this means: Boys tend to need more space in which to function while they are learning, need to move more during learning, and are generally more interested in and often better at spatial tasks than girls. This shows up more in science and technology classes (a crucial area for those of us teaching girls and working toward parity). Girls will often be tolerant when we ask them to sit still and be quiet at their desks while doing seat work, but they may not gravitate as quickly to spatial games, engineering or architectural designs, or computer languages. We may need to provide extra encouragement for them in these areas.

Sensory System   Females tend to process more sensory data across the senses. They tend to see better in more kinds of light, have better senses of hearing and smell, and to take in more information tactilely.

And this means: Girls will likely include more sensory detail in their writing and conversation. They will generally use more varied color in their artwork. Boys will tend to use fewer sensory descriptors in their writing, and this is an area in which those of us working with boys must be quite vigilant. Boys may also have a more difficult time hearing certain ranges of sound, especially from their usual, self-selected seat in the back of the room! This difference in the sensory system can result in differently designed classrooms in single-sex environments, as students want and need different surroundings to support learning. (See Chapters Five and Six for more information.)

Chemical Differences Between the Male and Female Brain

There are variations in the types and amounts of hormones and neurotransmitters that affect how boys and girls learn and interact; following are the main differences.

Testosterone   Males have significantly higher levels of testosterone, the male sex and aggression hormone, than females do. These levels contribute to boys' being more fidgety, more physical, and more spatially inclined. Male testosterone levels go up when boys "win" and decline when they "lose." Used appropriately, competition can be an important motivator in male learning environments. Although girls' testosterone levels don't tend to fluctuate during competition to the same degree that boys' levels do, research does show that girls who participate in healthy competitive activities tend to increase self-confidence and assertiveness.

Estrogen   Although both males and females have estrogen, a group of hormones generally referred to as the female sex hormone, levels tend to be significantly higher in the female system. Research indicates that estrogen may be related to aggression in girls and that levels are affected by the seasons, including daily hours of light. Lighting in a single-sex female environment can be designed with this in mind. In addition, elevated levels of body fat affect girls' estrogen levels, and researchers believe being overweight may be contributing to early onset of puberty.

Serotonin   This neurotransmitter is often referred to as the "feel-good" chemical because of its affect on mood. The male brain tends to have more serotonin, but because estrogen tends to facilitate processing of essential neurotransmitters, including serotonin, girls' systems process serotonin more efficiently, making them less likely to respond physically to stress. Once angry, boys have less access to serotonin to help them calm down and de-escalate. Single-sex environments can be conducive to helping both boys and girls learn positive, nonaggressive conflict management techniques that best fit them developmentally.

Dopamine   This neurotransmitter stimulates motivation and pleasure circuits in the brains of both girls and boys. Dopamine plays a major role in how the brain controls our physical movements—too little and we can't control our movements, too much and we might engage in unconscious movements such as tapping our pencil on the desk, jiggling our leg, picking at things. (Sound like a boy you've observed in your classroom?) Dopamine also plays a role in how information moves between areas of the brain, affecting memory, attention, and problem solving. In a boys-only classroom, previously unmotivated boys may experience increased dopamine as a result of teaching strategies that allow for more movement and experiential learning, potentially increasing dopamine and its positive effects.

Oxytocin   This chemical is often referred to as the "tend and befriend" hormone. Research has shown oxytocin to be involved in the formation of trust between people, and in social recognition and bonding. Females have significantly higher levels of oxytocin than males throughout life. As oxytocin promotes the development and maintenance of relationships, girls are much more biologically driven than boys to establish relationships and do whatever it takes to maintain them. This can result in unhealthy relationships among girls and in confusion in girl-boy relationships. In single-sex classrooms these issues can be addressed straightforwardly and often. This can be helpful to both boys and girls during puberty as it removes an area of great distraction that boys and girls experience quite differently.

Avoiding Stereotypes

As we explore the functioning of the "male" and "female" brain, it is important to remember that there are boys and girls for whom these descriptions will not fit. Boys are not all the same and girls are not all the same. Their brains are multifaceted, and they are capable of doing and being many things at many times. Though we will frequently generalize to provide a better understanding of gender-related differences, we caution against any inclination to stereotype either boys or girls. Biologists have proven that, along the spectrum of brain differences, there are huge variations within the parameters of the male and female brain. Although most girls tend toward the female end of the spectrum and most boys toward the male end, a number possess nearly equal qualities of both male and female brains. We refer to these boys and girls as "bridge brains," a term Michael coined for males and females who "bridge" the genders, from a brain-based point of view.

Finally, please keep in mind that although many of the chapters in this book have boy- or girl-specific titles, each chapter usually contains information about both boys and girls. In addition, many of the activities and strategies that appear in boys' chapters will also work well for girls, and vice versa. They will also work for coed classrooms, though there is a certain directness of application that may only be found in the single-sex environment.

Why Knowledge of Gender Differences Is Crucial for Teaching Boys

---

"It is not just that boys are falling behind girls. It's that boys themselves are falling behind their own functioning and doing worse than they did before."

—William S. Pollack, *The New Gender Gap*

Beginning several decades ago, it was reported that girls were being short-changed and disadvantaged in classrooms. To combat this, there was a push to get girls more interested in math and science. However, while that was happening, there were few, if any, programs to get boys more interested in academic areas where they tended to perform poorly, often reading and writing. The research now indicates that girls are closing the gap with boys in the areas of math and science, and also making strides in improving their technology skills. This earlier concern over the plight of girls has now shifted to a concern for boys, whom many view as "at risk" in today's schools. This concern is well documented in research that looks at boys' grades, test scores, disciplinary referrals, high school dropout rates, and college attendance and graduation statistics.

A WORRISOME GENDER GAP

- *Boys read far fewer books than girls.*
- *Boys receive as much as 70 percent of Ds and Fs given in schools.*
- *Boys account for up to 90 percent of classroom discipline referrals—more suspensions, more expulsions, and higher dropout rates.*
- *Boys are more likely to be diagnosed with ADHD.*
- *Boys are more likely to be enrolled in special education classes (approximately 70 percent of learning disability diagnoses are given to boys).*

- *For every 100 male students who receive bachelor's degrees in college, approximately 133 female students receive the same degree.*

- *Boys are more likely to be involved in high-risk behavior involving crime, alcohol, and drugs.*

- *Boys are far more likely to die from suicide attempts than girls (approximately five boys to every girl between the ages of 5 and 24).*

When the average boy enters kindergarten, developmentally he can be as much as a year and a half behind the girls in his class in reading and writing. His fine motor skills develop later than those of girls, making it more challenging for him to hold a pencil and write effectively. When he enters the classroom and sees that he is not as good at reading, writing, and drawing, it may cause him to think negatively about school and to begin feeling that school is not a very boy-friendly place. Yes, even as early as kindergarten, it seems that boys and school are often a poor match.

"Aaron, our bright five-year-old, is 'flunking' out of kindergarten and being placed in remedial reading and math programs. We're horrified and panic-stricken. Our Aaron, a happy, kind and extremely athletic child at home is sullen and disinterested at school. He HATES kindergarten because he says 'it's not fun.' Consequently, he passively refuses to do any school work or pay attention in class. He's not hyper, loud or disruptive, he just tunes out the teacher, is joyless and falling further behind. Everyone is baffled. We didn't believe it until we observed it ourselves."

—Aaron's mom

Boys are nevertheless placed in classrooms with girls and expected to learn the same material within the same span of time. Thus, beginning at a very young age, boys—who are far more inclined to be running, playing, and building—are expected to sit in a classroom for six or more hours. Then, when these boys act out or fail to do well in school, they are often labeled as ADHD, taken out of the regular classroom, and placed in special education programs or given medication, such as Ritalin, to help them focus.

There are, of course, boys who do suffer from ADHD, and for many of them medication will be extremely helpful. But can the numbers be as high as they seem to be? Over four million American boys are on Ritalin and the United States uses 80 percent of the world's Ritalin. Are some boys being diagnosed with brain disorders for merely acting out their boy energy in classrooms that assign more value to sitting still and being quiet?

As boys move into high school and then college we continue to see that they are less motivated and engaged in school than girls. One concerned father wrote, "My son is now a junior in high school. I can see his intelligence and his wit, but neither is reflected in his grades. He has gotten several Fs in his high school career and one of my fears is that he will not be properly prepared for college or the world after if we keep going this way. I want him to graduate with his class but that appears to be in jeopardy. He just doesn't seem to care about succeeding in school at all." It is boys like this who might well benefit from a single-sex school and an environment designed to help boys thrive.

DID YOU KNOW? BOYS ARE FALLING BEHIND IN SCHOOL

- Boys outnumber girls in high school sports participation, but girls greatly outnumber them in every other extracurricular activity, from student government to school newspapers and academic clubs.

- Boys are more likely to express a strong dislike for school or state that they find their courses dull.

- More than one-third of male high school students say they seldom (or never) find their work to be "meaningful or important," and approximately the same number say that what they are learning will have little or no importance to them later in life.

- High school female students take 54 percent of Advanced Placement (AP) exams, and this gap continues to grow.

- Only 66 percent of male high school seniors say they will "definitely" graduate from a two- or four-year college program, compared to 82 percent of females. Likewise, only 16 percent of these males plan to "definitely" attend

As we make decisions to find ways to educate our boys for success, we develop methods that work better for them in environments that fit the male brain. These environments allow them to channel their energy and aggressive natures in positive directions. By respecting boys for who they are and guiding them in developmentally appropriate ways, we can more easily teach them and make a positive difference in their lives.

Single-sex classrooms can be one of the innovative environments that fully understands a boy's developmental trajectory, male learning style, and male needs. The success experienced in many boys-only classes and schools today is in large part due to vigilance on the part of these boys' teachers to create environments that fit the male brain.

Why Knowledge of Brain Differences Is Crucial for Teaching Girls

"A girl's increasing stress and anxiety response at puberty may even be related to the formation of cliques and clubs. In fact, the formation of cliques may be the result of her stress response."

—Louann Brizendine, *The Female Brain*

Generally, girls are better able to meet expectations in the traditional classroom. They learn to read earlier and tend to achieve better, particularly in the early grades. They find it easier to listen, pay attention, speak, and write, and they deal with interpersonal relationships better than boys do. Although girls also love to move and explore within their learning environments, they can tolerate sitting while learning much more easily than boys. The female brain, with its ability to pick up more sensory detail, enables girls to better decipher the expectations of the teacher, and so they are frequently better equipped than boys to be successful in the classroom.

However, as young girls progress beyond the early grades into pre-adolescence, they begin to experience considerable stress and issues relating to self-esteem and confidence, both in and out of school. Many of the stressors that begin to surface for girls happen as early as third or fourth grade, and may have their greatest impact throughout the middle and early high school years when girls are frequently less confident.

"Stress? Well, I'd say peer pressure, homework, lack of sleep, parents. A lot of things are stressful."

—Chloe, 10th grade girl

Adolescence is also a time when girls begin to face greater challenges in academic subjects that require them to employ their spatial skills and understanding, especially as they deal with higher-level math, hands-on science, and technology. Then, as puberty hits, their bodies begin to change rapidly. Their gross motor skills are generally less developed than those of boys, and they may feel more awkward, clumsy, and less skilled in athletic endeavors than they once did, or as compared to boys at this stage of development. Greatly influenced by the media and by their peers, girls are likely to begin worrying more about their physical appearance. As they begin to notice boys and care more about what boys think, some girls may become quieter, especially during coed classroom discussions. In general, girls do not wish to appear too smart in front of boys, so they may inadvertently "dumb themselves down."

> *In general, girls do not wish to appear too smart in front of boys, so they may inadvertently "dumb themselves down."*

Simultaneously, a girl's relationships can invade her learning. Finding her place and feeling that she belongs to the social group of her choice are very important for a girl, but dealing with the ever-changing social dynamics can prove daunting. In the face of these challenges, girls often find it difficult to make the best decisions. Relationships with parents are among the issues that can become problematic, as adolescent girls find themselves pushing away the very people who may have the most potential to help them.

It's important to note that when trying to cope with all of these stressors, girls typically respond differently than boys do. A girl is much more likely than a boy to internalize her problems as "her failure." A typical reaction might be, "I'm just not smart enough to learn math." A boy is more likely to blame an external circumstance, with statements such as "Coach won't let me play enough." Even though a girl's verbal skills may be strong, she may suffer in silence, not choosing to admit that there is a problem. When this occurs, a girl delays some of the means by which she might otherwise get help. First, it may take longer for an adult to discover that there is a problem. Second, it will take longer for her to discover that many of her female peers are struggling with the same issues. Without these adults and peers, she has little opportunity to actually deal with the problem that she faces.

Unchecked, the escalating stress may reach a level that causes some girls to act out. With their stronger verbal skills, girls are capable of quickly taking a stressful situation to a new, more harmful level, resulting in unhealthy drama, hurtful gossip, or even relational aggression, a form of female bullying. In a few cases, as girls deal with many layers of stress, becoming more troubled and less confident, they may react with more dramatic consequences—experiencing depression, starving themselves, cutting themselves, and becoming violent to others—in an effort to deal with life's challenges and drops in their self-esteem. Though most girls are successfully navigating their way through adolescence in both their personal and academic lives, some are definitely not.

A girls-only classroom can provide a place for learning that is free of competition with boys, the need for boys' attention, and overemphasis on physical appearance. It can be a place where girls get involved, ask important questions, and gain the confidence to excel, especially in areas where they may previously have been challenged. For somewhat different reasons, but with the same brain-based analysis behind it, the girls-only classroom can be just as helpful for girls as is the boys-only classroom for boys.

SUMMARY OF POTENTIAL BRAIN-BASED BENEFITS TO SINGLE-SEX CLASSROOMS

Doug MacIsaac, professional development school coordinator at the Nina B. Hollis Institute for Educational Reform at Stetson University, has devoted much of his career to studying the pros and cons of single-sex classes. He utilizes brain-based research to train teachers and has worked closely with Woodward Elementary School. Here is a partial summary of potential benefits Doug has observed in single-sex classrooms.

1. Many girls may be more likely to try new things when boys are not around. This is especially true for things that are usually thought of as "boy" areas (such as math, science, technology).

2. Greater learning can occur when girls are grouped with other girls. Girls enjoy working collaboratively and will naturally break into groups of three or four to work on an assignment. However, studies have shown that pairing a girl with a boy on a task can reduce the girl's performance by as much as 50 percent. Boys are frequently more competitive, especially with spatial tasks. Thus pairing boys and girls together can create challenges for girls' everyday learning.

3. Girls can often talk about emotions better than boys. They find it easier to share their feelings. They enjoy books about relationships, whereas boys tend to prefer action books. Separating the genders for language arts can make discussions easier for both sexes.

4. Role-playing activities can often work better for girls and boys when they are done in single-sex groups.

5. Navigational tasks are handled in different parts of the brain. For girls it is in the cerebral cortex, the same general area that is responsible for language. For boys it is the hippocampus. This has significance for learning topics requiring spatial understanding, such as geometry, number theory, and algebra. Girls may tend

to verbally process the learning more than boys, and boys may be more inclined to just charge ahead with the task without processing. Girls often feel more free to pursue these skills when boys are not around.

6. Many boys feel unable to compete with girls verbally, but can flourish verbally in boys-only environments, where expectations are based more on boys' verbal strengths and preferences.

7. Girls often enjoy a quieter classroom than boys. Some boys need a classroom that is loud and lively to keep their brains stimulated to learn effectively. This can feel disruptive to girls.

Added Benefits

Though the enhancement of learning has been the driving motivation behind single-sex instruction, there have been related benefits in the areas of discipline and overall school climate. Conclusive, quantifiable research on the effects of single-sex instruction is difficult to find, but anecdotal results are available from numerous schools. Many report dramatic improvements in academic testing for some students. Others report a significant reduction in discipline referrals, or an improvement in school climate, with happier, more engaged students and teachers. Still others report positive results in all of these areas.

"Whether in the heartland of the United States or the heart of Africa, single-sex classes provide a compelling way to accommodate the educational needs of [children]."

—Dr. Frances Spielhagen, *Debating Single-Sex Education: Separate and Equal?*

WRAPPING UP THE MAIN POINTS

At the institutional level, schools may choose to pursue single-sex instruction for many reasons, including:

- Improving test scores
- Meeting standards of accountability
- Decreasing disciplinary problems
- Helping students who are failing and falling further behind
- More fully engaging top learners
- Energizing a school community
- Simply offering a choice

Whatever the initial reasons, schools may later discover additional benefits, particularly when the instructional model is designed to provide a nurturing environment in which members of each gender are able to explore their individual identities and interests and to pursue their potential in an atmosphere of mutual respect. These goals are best accomplished when teachers and schools promote self-expression, student interest, empowerment, and full participation, while encouraging teachers to work in ways that are nonjudgmental, sensitive to gender issues, and in keeping with the latest brain research.

PART TWO

Setting Up and Maintaining Your Single-Sex Program

Schools that use gender as a lens to understand boys and girls on their own terms create opportunities that open them up, not close them down, and that makes them feel good about boys and girls learning new things. These schools foster a sense of being in control responsibly. Some exist now. Many more could become those places if they would consider giving boys and girls a chance to take time out from each other—to learn to be who they are and achieve their potential in all of their gendered and human glory.

—Lorraine Garnett Ward, former dean, Wellesley College

Setting Up a Single-Sex Instructional Program

The American tradition favors pluralism, diversity and choice. There should be coed schools for those who want them and single-sex schools for those who prefer an environment free of the pressures of the dating game.

—Diane Ravitch, "Why Not a Girls School?"

If you, your school, and your community are exploring the single-sex approach as the best response to your specific school improvement goals, you may have already made a list of logistical difficulties that arise when teachers or schools decide to transition to single-sex classes. A number of the challenges associated with such a transition are gathered in the following questions. These are the key topics that schools we've worked with have kept in the forefront as they investigate transitioning to some form of single-sex education. Because you can expect to be questioned by community members or staff about most of these, it is useful to put together a leadership team that will steward the transition to single-sex classrooms. The questioning that occurs during the  exploratory process as well as the ultimate implementation of the program can be a healthy form of transition—by asking and answering questions very practically, your school and community come together to develop both a mutual buy-in for single-sex instruction and a logistical smoothness at school and at home.

QUESTIONS TO ANSWER AS YOU TRANSITION TO SINGLE-SEX INSTRUCTION

The following are eight questions that generally arise as schools and communities are setting up their transition to a single-sex program.

1. How do the suggested benefits of single-sex instruction specifically relate to the circumstances in our school?

To answer this, you will need to gather and disseminate data in your school or district regarding learning and achievement gaps associated with gender in different age groups (elementary, middle, high school). You will also need to disseminate information regarding the "solution" that single-sex classes can bring to gender gaps. This book provides success data that you can use to make your case to your teachers, administrators, and community.

2. Which grades or classes will be involved?

One way to answer this question is simply to plan on one or two classes transitioning over to single-sex. Math, science, and language arts are most common, but any class can become single-sex. If you can successfully gather data on a few single-sex classes operating in your school during the first year of transition, then you can then build a stronger case for even more classes making the switch. Success data from your own school or district is powerful!

3. How will decisions be made regarding student recruitment for single-sex classes?

In your staff meetings, you will need to put recruitment standards on the agenda for discussion and policy decision making. A specific written policy, suited to your school and community, will later need to be distributed to both parents and teachers. In regard to student placement in single-sex classes, you will want to consider all of the following: student performance, aptitude, behavior, classroom dynamics, and parent requests. Again, be sure to include any other important factors that may pertain specifically to your school. In your official policy, make sure parents are well aware of these issues.

4. How will our school make sure that single-sex instruction does not disadvantage some students socially?

If you and your colleagues feel that separating boys and girls may create a vacuum of male-female interaction, other social opportunities will need to compensate. This issue is generally not of concern to schools that only utilize single-sex classes in certain core areas—it is an issue for single-sex schools that separate boys and girls, at different locations, for all classes.

5. How do you prepare for opposition to your single-sex plan?

Discuss in your leadership team how adding single-sex classes affects the four core groups involved: students, teachers, parents, and administrators. Which groups or individuals in your school or community will find it difficult to buy in to this option? Which groups will see it as a welcome change? Which people or groups are apt to be the source and the nature of the strongest opposition? Whenever you go out into your school and community to investigate support for the single-sex option, or if you are transitioning to it right now, it is crucial to promulgate written statements that preemptively answer opposition issues. As this workbook proceeds, you will see a number of these oppositional questions addressed, and you'll find language you can use, should you choose to, in your memos to constituent groups.

6. How will the transition to single-sex affect school logistics, such as scheduling, classroom space, class size, and teacher assignments?

Each logistical issue needs careful attention so that the transition is smooth. Administrators and teachers generally like to come together in a set of preparation meetings to refine logistics and assign different issues to be resolved. Quite often, too, this leadership team discovers that logistical issues are not too cumbersome at all.

7. How will we train teachers for teaching in single-sex classes? What are the costs involved?

Teacher training in male-female brain and learning differences, which includes classroom strategies for teaching boys and girls separately, is critical to the success of single-sex programs. For the best transition into this program, training should happen before single-sex classes actually begin in the school. When an untrained teacher is placed in a classroom with twenty-five or more boys *or* girls, he or she may find aspects of single-sex instruction overwhelming, and the program may not meet expected results. However, when schools make training a priority, teachers will be more prepared and every child who participates in single-sex classrooms will benefit.

8. How will we disseminate information to school families? Will parent education be a part of the plan? If so, how do we get parents involved?

Parent involvement is crucial to the success of single-sex programming. When you involve parents, both as representatives on the leadership team itself and as a constituency in constant communication with the school, you ensure parental buy-in. Under federal guidelines, single-sex programs in public schools are voluntary, as are the few schools that are completely single-sex; therefore, parental buy-in can make or break a program.

As you move forward, make sure to meet to address these concerns and to determine what steps are necessary in your school or district in order to get final approval. If you find legal issues related to implementing single-sex classes, deal with them right away. Throughout the rest of this book, we will provide you with information you can use in your leadership meetings, your parent outreach, your logistical transition, and your pursuit of knowledge regarding legal and social issues pertaining to the single-sex classroom.

FOCUSING ON SCHOOL NEEDS: TRANSITIONING YOUR SCHOOL EFFECTIVELY

As you consider a single-sex program in your school, or as you move toward it, you will probably find yourself answering the eight key questions we just mentioned via three major foci: the school's needs, the teachers' needs, and the parents' needs. Through this triumvirate, most schools find they are accomplishing the ultimate (and first) goal of all their efforts: meeting students' needs.

Leadership for the Single-Sex Program

"I knew that I wanted to be the principal of the single-gender all girls school in Atlanta after the first face-to-face interview with the panel from APS. I was interested in this position because it was the one thing that was not part of my educational experience in the twenty-nine years I spent in the New York City school system. I love a challenge and I love experiencing new roles and responsibilities. I followed the progress of the Harlem Young Women's Leadership Academy and the Oprah Winfrey Leadership Academy and

became interested in being part of a school like the two that I consider to be extremely successful."

—Melody Morgan, principal, Coretta Scott King Young
Women's Leadership Academy, Atlanta, Georgia

For any new school program to be successful, good leadership is crucial—not only to put the program in place, but also to manage the program in ways that confirm its importance.

In the initial phases, principals who pursue the model of single-sex instruction must provide focus and direction for the school, leading through data-driven goals with an unwavering emphasis on improving student learning. Demonstrating a personal investment in defining and shaping the program, they must also be willing to share the responsibility for gathering and organizing the research, and for designing and implementing the specific program chosen. As described in greater detail

below, principals are also likely to have primary responsibility for the hiring and training of the individuals critical to the success of the program—the teachers.

Later, following implementation, principals continue to be an important part of the process of reviewing, improving, and building upon the program's success. This includes not just managing the time and financial resources devoted to the program, but also maintaining a coherent agenda and creating a culture of support and reasonable expectation within the school community.

Determining Which Age Groups in Your School Would Benefit from Single-Sex Instruction

As the leadership team explores incorporating the single-sex option, an early focus will be on determining which age group will find it most beneficial—students in elementary, middle, or high school (or all age groups)?

Mary Richards, an elementary school parent, wrote us this e-mail: "My fifth grade daughters have certainly felt less intimidated without boys in science and math classes. Both have done much better this year. They like that their teachers relate their learning to girl interests. One teacher talks honestly with the girls about their bodies and personal hygiene; and I am amazed at how well the girls in my daughter's class respond. The girls' teachers also inspire them in terms of being athletes and taking care of their health."

Elementary School   Some schools choose to implement single-sex instruction at the elementary level, often starting in the early grades where students are just beginning to read and write. As discussed in Chapter One, the main reason is that boys and girls generally enter school at different developmental levels of readiness in terms of verbal, spatial, and fine-motor skills, as well as maturity. At the elementary level, the girls either are already ahead or quickly outpace the boys in reading and writing skills. When girls and boys are taught separately in the early grades, it means that the ranges of ability within each class will usually be narrower, allowing the teacher to more easily meet the students' needs and move them along at a faster, more uniform pace. Generally, this plays out in reading-writing for boys, and math-science for girls.

Regarding middle school, math-science teacher Kevin McManus wrote, "In my single-sex boys' math class, the boys benefit from no longer feeling the need to impress girls with ridiculous behavior, but they still jockey for position within boy hierarchy. They are doing better in math, working more cooperatively and wanting to teach each other."

Middle School   Some schools choose to start single-sex programs during the middle school years for many of the same reasons we described for elementary school. In addition, middle schools in particular are also looking to minimize the social, emotional, and romantic distractions that naturally begin during early adolescence. Separating boys and girls can make for more comfortable classrooms, where both genders are more willing to take risks, speak up, contribute answers, express uncertainties, and ask questions.

"Teaching young adolescents in the coed classroom is like teaching multilingual classes—with several languages going on at once, the boy language, the girl language, and the teacher language. Everyone is thinking differently and reacting differently to information, so the benefits of separating boys and girls to cut down on the natural communication differences make sense."

—John Zazzaro, high school history teacher

High School   More coed public high schools are expressing interest in and piloting single-sex programs. High schools often begin single-sex instruction by separating boys and girls for math and English composition or literature courses. Educators experienced with single-sex instruction at the high school level recognize that students in these programs benefit from taking a greater breadth of courses. Girls are more willing to take nontraditional higher-level math, physics, and technology courses, and more boys take courses in the arts and languages. Overall, these schools report that students in these programs can become more engaged in learning, finding their classes enjoyable and the curriculum more relevant to their needs as learners.

FOCUSING ON TEACHERS: SELECTING TEACHERS FOR THE SINGLE-SEX PROGRAM

Curt Green, principal of the B.E.S.T. Academy in Atlanta, shared his vision for the qualities he wanted to see in teachers at the new single-sex school:

- *Passionate—they enjoy teaching boys*
- *Flexible—they have a student-centered teaching style, and are willing to allow the students to have ownership in their own learning*
- *Technologically savvy—they incorporate technology into the curriculum*
- *Nontraditional—they are less focused on paper-and-pencil, more hands-on learning along with student presentations*
- *Humorous—they can laugh and be laughed at*
- *Theatrical—they can make the lesson come alive*
- *Relaxed—they enjoy movement and noise in the classroom—allow students to move freely and discuss information without being a distraction to the teacher*

Teacher selection is vital to the success of single-sex programs. The teachers who are matched with students in these programs need to "fit" the classes they teach. The principal will usually be the person who selects, hires, oversees training, and evaluates these teachers. When placing existing faculty into single-sex classes and when hiring new teachers for a single-sex program, the principal should consider each candidate's awareness of and commitment to gender-based learning. The initial and perhaps most important question to ask potential teachers in a proposed single-sex school is why they want to work in the program. You are asking them: **What is your personal motivation for wanting to be part of this single-sex teaching opportunity?**

Here is a sampling of teacher responses that reveal a sense of optimism and high expectations regarding single-sex options. Optimism and reachable, high expectations are crucial to the success of single-sex instructional programs. These responses are from teachers at two new single-sex public middle schools in Georgia:

- Mine is very simple. I love the challenge of new projects and the prospect of how I can make a positive difference as well as grow professionally through the experience.

- My expectation for the girls is that they will come to accept education as a primary personal need that will enhance them as individuals. I expect that they will grow expressively, socially, academically, morally, and emotionally. I believe not having to compete for the attention of the opposite sex nor prove themselves socially among their own sex will give them a new focus. I expect that their course work will be more meaningful as a result.

- I want to work in a school that is going to implement positive programs, which research has proven successful in urban communities.

- My motivation for wanting to be a part of this single-gender school pilot is truly my belief that I can make the most significant difference in this type of setting. Our children deserve a focused and tailored education; a curriculum that involves the whole person. In addition to this, I really want to be a part of something new and fresh and something that I believe in.

- I have firsthand experience with the positive impacts of single-gender classrooms. Attending an all women's college focused my attention on education and gave me confidence to study math and economics. I also have firsthand experience teaching single-gender classes.

- I believe that the boys will become more focused and that a single-gender setting will ultimately reduce the distractions that come as a result of adolescence and peer pressure. I expect the boys to grow to become honorable and mighty students in their endeavors.

- While working on my educational specialist degree in brain research and instructional leadership, I gained a new interest in how boys and girls learn differently. When I implemented the strategies into my classes, I began to see the significant difference in the learning styles of each gender. When the opportunity was presented to become a part of this wonderful academic institution, I pounced on it.

Hiring and teacher selection conversations need to include the prospective teachers' willingness to pursue training in brain-based gender instruction, to stay up-to-date on related research by reading books and articles on the topic, and to incorporate proven techniques to maximize learning in the single-sex classroom. Teachers in this program must be willing to monitor student progress through observation and achievement data and reflect on what did and did not work for boys or for girls.

"When looking for teachers to lead our single-gender classrooms, I wanted the teacher who relates to students and develops relationships that go far beyond state curriculum standards. I wanted that teacher who understands that students do not care how much you know, until they know you care about them. The teacher must have the capabilities of establishing a camaraderie between themselves and the students they teach. I was fortunate to find two such teachers already employed by the middle school."

—Al Darby, high school principal, Georgia

What Teachers Have Said About Their Programs: Challenging Your Own Teachers

The following pages are journal entries from two teachers. Roger Chaney is a sixth-grade teacher of a pilot all-boys class at Desert Heights Elementary School, a public K–6 school in Reno, Nevada. Dorie Jensen teaches an all-girls sixth-grade class at the same school. These two teachers kept journals during the first year of single-sex education in their school.

You may also note that the journal from the male teacher, Roger, is much shorter than the journal from the female teacher, Dorie. Brain differences are at work, whether in childhood or adulthood. In over 80 percent of cases, when we have read journals from male teachers, they have been shorter than journals of female teachers.

We thank these teachers for sharing their reflections, allowing others to consider—even in advance—the challenges and possibilities that exist when teaching single-sex classes. By publishing these, we hope that prospective teachers will feel more informed and ready to carefully consider their own excitement or hesitation regarding this option. Prior to committing, they should make sure that working in this kind of environment is what they really want.

Finally, if you are a principal, share these journals with prospective teachers. The insights of Roger and Dorie are fascinating and very useful for discussion.

Excerpts from Roger Chaney's Journal Regarding Boys-Only Classes

August 28, 2007

Going into the school year, after reading through a couple of the recommended books from Dr. Studer, I am still curious as to how I am going to relate, address, direct my new class of Extraordinary Gentlemen. I imagined that I would, roughly, communicate the same way I would communicate with a mixed-sex class. Our class will be set up with tables to begin the year. I have never grouped my students this early in the past. I am curious how this will work with boys.

September 17, 2007

I find that I communicate differently with the boys than I thought I would. The language I use with them is short, succinct, and without discussion or much explanation. The boys' conversations are about things they have done, things they plan to do, not about their relationships with one another.

October 1, 2007

I am finding that writing tends to be a chore for the boys. I don't know if this is something that comes with sixth grade in general, or just with the boys in my class. Small-group work is beginning to become more productive, with discussions being more focused on assigned task, and less on what they watched on TV the night before. PE has been great. Competition with boys tends to be focused on the task at hand (shoot, pass, score). I believe the development of team-work early in the year is critical to the success of group work through-out the year. The boys are hard on each other, as well as themselves, for not performing well in a sport. We have discussed the time and effort it takes to become good at anything. It is different for everyone, and comes in different forms.

December 3, 2007

Is it a part of being a boy at this age? Where does it become tangible, again, when you do something that is not allowed in school, you get in trouble? Shooting a rubber band, not doing your homework, etc. It isn't always the usual suspects that find themselves in this position. I am finding that a growing number of the boys are beginning to seri-ously take some responsibility for their academic path. Homework is being done on time, classwork is given more attention and overall quality of their work is improving. One of my goals with the guys is to have them find some intrinsic value, within their academic lifetime that will be their fire to keep them going after any academic endeavor. Yikes.

January 27, 2008

My initial perception of attitude change in the lads (returning from the holiday break) was confirmed when I returned to the class after they had a substitute for two days. A small group of boys made it a point to be completely disrespectful to the substitute by disregarding his multiple requests for them to be quiet and to get back on task. When I addressed the boys that chose to be disrespectful, I immedi-ately turned their recesses into community service at school for the month of February. One day of discipline for this kind of behavior, at this age, is not enough. Trust is a two-way street that takes time to repair. I want them to know that I believe that they can take care of themselves and the class. Is removing their perceived privileges the best road to take?

February 20, 2008

Two of the three boys that were addressed have changed their behavior dramatically, to the better. Homework is coming in more consistently, and their quality of writing has improved through their expression and creativity.

April 4, 2008

As we enter our final quarter of the school year, I attempt to take a step back from my class and myself as a teacher to reflect on the past eight months in the classroom. Since this is my first year teaching sixth grade as well as teaching all boys I have continually questioned whether things are happening the way they are because I am working with sixth graders, or they are a result of the sixth graders being all boys. Not only am I getting a better feel for how to address boys as boys, but when to address them as learners. The strategies we have been presented with, as a result of the research that has been conducted in the field of single-sex education, have been insightful and helpful. Revisiting the strategies that we were presented with at the beginning of the year now has an applicable place within my classroom design and management. I will continue to have reading and math in the morning, in order to make the best use of the boys' ability to concentrate and employ reading comprehension strategies. The effects of a mid-morning break (between reading and math) have been mostly positive from the fact that the boys were less inclined to be off task in the morning if they knew they had a break where they could visit with their classmates before lunch. I will continue to have a mid-morning break next year. The way I will present any subject in the afternoon, next year, will be in the fashion of group-oriented projects and activities. The energy level of the boys after coming in from almost an hour on the playground has been far too high to expect them to sit down and direct their attention to something far more sedentary than what they were experiencing out on the playground. As for the way I communicate, in general, with the boys, I plan to focus more along the guidelines of the Less Talk Lesson Plans. I will also begin our day as a whole class discussion (Tribes), in a group circle. We will discuss how the day is going to look from my perspective, and open the floor to anyone who would like to talk about the way they are coming into their day at school. I am looking forward to the year to come. These are exciting times.

Excerpts from Dorie Jensen's Journal Regarding Girls-Only Classes

September 21, 2007

I realized today how these girls seem willing to try things they aren't good at. They're not afraid to try new things or even to fail. I wouldn't have seen that in the past, with a mixed class; certainly not this early in the year.

October 10, 2007

I had a great conference. There were several "Aha" moments for me. The first one was when they talked about how we tell little boys to be quiet and good, like little Susie. I always saw the effect on the boy, but until this conference, I didn't see the effect on the girls. It makes them lose their voice. They only think they're good when they're being quiet.

We had to substitute in the kindergarten this morning. I definitely saw the value in separating the genders that early. We're really doing a disservice to these boys at this age.

October 22, 2007

While we're doing a lesson on fractions using pattern blocks, most of the girls INSIST on sorting and counting all the different shapes in their bags. For some reason, they seem unable to go on to the actual lesson until that's done.

They are very cooperative and helpful to one another. They help the others in their group without being asked. It's all very cooperative.

I also hear the phrases, "Let's try . . ." and "I think it goes like this . . ."

They definitely work well together without distraction of boys. I even heard "I messed up on . . ." and there wasn't any problem with admitting it.

November 8, 2007

We had PE with the UNR [University of Nevada Reno] students again today and they made very interesting observations. I would not have been able to see it. They also worked with Ms. Enteles' [coed] class and they noticed that the girls in my class were much more competitive while the girls in the other class "mostly stood back and let the boys dominate." I think that's significant.

November 20, 2007

It's going to be hard to go back to teaching math with a mixed class. For some reason, this is much less stressful. I can't really put my finger on it, but there's a lot less angst. I know that's a strange word, but it's the one that fit. I hope the scores show real improvement. Their attitudes have certainly improved. My instinct tells me it's because there doesn't seem to be as much pressure, and I'm not quite sure why that is. I'll work on it.

December 17, 2007

I had an "Aha" moment this weekend. In a quiet moment I was thinking about the class this year. We had just finished a math module and taken the finals, etc. I was reflecting on how that went and how different it is teaching in an all-female class. The whole climate surrounding math is different. It's calmer and more relaxed somehow. I couldn't figure this out because I'm basically doing the exact same thing I always do—same curriculum, same manipulatives, same activities. It's still student-driven instruction.

And that was the difference. Girls process math differently and in an all-girl class, they're able to do that processing their way. All of the pressure of combining styles is gone and they feel free to actually try and understand math without being successful the first time. They realize they can *not* get it right away and still be allowed to work on it.

One of the female strategies that's really worked has been to do everything visually with them . . . and not just visually, but describing and explaining every step. It has seemed to work for many of the girls. There are still girls who aren't getting it, but they can at least repeat the steps.

I know there's a lot more work to do, but it really has been amazing. I've really enjoyed it. And now I think I've figured out why.

January 10, 2008

We started a new science unit yesterday, so I set up the microscopes for today. I heard the most interesting comment from a student when she saw them. She actually said, "Why are we using the microscopes?" I answered we needed them for our science unit. She replied, "We can't use microscopes." I asked her why, but was not prepared for her answer, which was, "Because we're girls."

I honestly didn't know how to answer. I asked her why she thought that and she really couldn't tell me. She just didn't think girls could use microscopes.

I'm going to get her some books or articles on women who use microscopes. I don't know if it's really something she thinks, or if she was trying to get out of doing the labs.

January 14, 2008

I was talking to the music teacher today after school and she told me about an interesting observation she had last week. Each class had to use the music room one day when their room was painted and she would generally spend the first 15–30 minutes in her room. She told me she noticed a big difference between the mixed class and the single gender classes. She had really noticed it after my class (the last one).

She said that the atmosphere between the classes was totally different. I asked her in what way and she said that in both single-gender class there was less gossip and showing off and that the students seemed more tuned in to the teacher. I thought it was an interesting observation. I asked her if the gossip part was missing in my class of all girls, and she said it definitely was. That's why she noticed it. I think that's kind of strange. Girls are known for being gossips, but she didn't even see it. She said she's noticed a definite difference in music class, but it was very clear when all of the students were in their class.

January 29, 2008

Math with girls is so completely different than math in a mixed class. We're working on percentages and finding parts of a whole number, i.e. four-fifths of 125. These girls are able to stay completely on task while they're working it out. When I go from group to group they're helping one another and reinforcing their learning. I even heard an excited, "I get it now!" That's music to a teacher's ears, but I realized, I seldom hear that in a mixed class. There could be several reasons for that, but I'm glad I got to hear it today.

January 31, 2008

This really isn't anything academic, but I was so stunned when I heard it I wanted to put it in my journal. The girls were just coming in for the day and getting settled when one of my snootier girls said to another girl, so everyone could hear, "You're so pretty! You should cut your bangs like that again." They were looking at an old picture in the pocket of her binder.

I know girls may talk like that out of class, but I've never heard anything like that in class. And the coolest part was that she said it to a VERY shy, quiet girl. The comment, and the way she said it, could have made that girl's day, or month even.

February 27, 2008

We had half the boys in class today because there was no sub for Mr. Chaney. It was an "interesting" experience. The differences were amazing, or I'm just noticing them more. The girls in my class definitely noticed them too, and very early in the day.

The boys were noisy and played around on their own. I don't usually have to be on top of the girls about that kind of stuff anymore, so I wasn't used to doing it. I can usually make the assignment, go over the expectations, and then let the class go while I work with individual students or small groups. With the boys in the classroom, the girls were still able to work that way, but the boys couldn't do it at all.

Another difference everyone noticed was that no one wanted to read out loud or volunteer to answer anything. I usually have plenty of volunteers to do those things, but with the boys here, no one, boy or girl, wanted to do it.

I asked the girls later why they didn't speak up, and wasn't surprised that I already knew the answer. We had a talk about speaking up next year when they're with boys. They have to speak up, not just for questions, but also for the answers. No one should be embarrassed to if they know something, or if they don't.

After today, I really want to trade with Mr. Chaney and teach the boys for a day or so. I really want to see the differences after this year.

Training Teachers for Results

Good teachers make all the difference, regardless of the makeup of the class. They believe that all students can learn, and each day they strive to positively influence and shape the minds of the young people in their charge. They enter their classrooms with detailed plans designed to teach the curriculum, and they end many days feeling successful. However, on other days, they realize they did not make as much progress as they had hoped. In many cases this may result from the instructional techniques they employed rather than the knowledge they were trying to impart. Gender difference is a factor that needs to be considered as teachers assess how their students receive and understand new information. The more teachers know and understand about the workings of the human brain and the ways in which gender influences learning, the more successful they will be with their daily objective of developing the minds of their students.

DID YOU KNOW? STUDENTS CAN BOND QUITE WELL WITH TEACHERS IN THEIR SINGLE-SEX CLASSES

Here are examples of how girls feel about teachers in their single-sex classes:

- I get a lot of attention and more individual help from teachers in my single-sex classes. I got a lot more help in math this year, which I needed.
- I like that we can talk to our female teachers about girl things.
- Before, I was afraid to say, "I don't get it." Now the teacher makes me feel fine saying it.

How some boys feel about teachers in their single-sex classes:

- I think I get a lot of good attention in my all-boys' class.
- I like single-sex because the teachers make us more free to be ourselves in class.
- Mr. Hayes taught us totally different this year. Since the girls were not around, I did not worry so much when I said something that was a little off. Neither did Mr. Hayes. He understands boys and he is cool!

Even in light of an ever-increasing body of research over the past twenty years, few colleges and universities provide their students with specific knowledge concerning the ways in which boys and girls learn differently. The vast majority of teachers are not trained in this content area—many of today's most experienced teachers were educated to consider gender as simply a social function. For this reason, they tend to treat the boys and the girls in their classes relatively the same. As educators strive to maximize learning, we need a commitment from schools of education across the nation to train future teachers in the biology of learning, incorporating an understanding of brain-based gender differences.

Certainly, single-sex teachers need to be trained and well equipped to apply gender-specific tools in their classrooms. This will help them develop innovative ways to reach the minds of boys and girls.

Although these future goals will not address the lack of training for current teachers, there are resources and programs to provide such training for teachers, helping them learn strategies to address closing the gender gap for boys and girls, improving overall school performance, decreasing disciplinary referrals, and helping schools meet mandated performance standards.

Do Boys Need to Be Taught by Men and Girls By Women?

Some believe that it is best for boys to be taught by men and for girls to be taught by women, and in some cases this is true, especially for those children who need same-sex gender role models. However, it is not necessary that this always occur. Both genders gain from experiencing a variety of teachers with different teaching styles. Boys can benefit in significant ways from female teachers who actually prefer and do work better with boys, and girls can benefit from having a male teacher who is sensitive to girls and their issues. The bottom line is that all kids need the best possible teacher at every stage of their educational journey.

"Because I want the same things from both my boys and girls groups—namely, for them to be challenged and to succeed—I find myself using different sides of my brain to achieve the same results. Girls seem to respond better when I listen more, and when I keep myself as calm and reassuring as I can be. Boys, when having difficulty, respond to direct, sometimes loud and confrontational encouragement. Both groups respond well to humor—but the girls seem to laugh at my jokes more out of politeness than because they're funny!"

—Chris McGrath, middle school language arts and
social studies teacher

FOCUSING ON PARENTS: BRINGING PARENTS INTO THE DIALOGUE

Parental energy and buy-in is crucial to the success of single-sex programs. Here are some key areas of focus as you introduce single-sex innovations to parents.

Making Your Case to Your School and to Parents

A principal in Georgia told us: "As I stood in the hall during the change of class, several of the sixth grade boys came up to me individually to tell me that their grades were better than ever without being with girls. Two of those boys said that they had straight As for the first time ever. Those same two boys said that their moms said that they could never go to class with girls again!"

This is the kind of positive comment that you may want to collect from other schools and from this book as you build your case for parents. It can be quite beneficial to mix these anecdotal quotes with success data. As you put these statements and the success data in writing, key in on certain powerful community members who can help you make your case to the community. If you haven't already, now might be the time to bring some of these people onto a single-sex classes leadership team. Often, these parents will have their collective finger on the pulse of the community—they will know the kinds of objections that can arise, and what kind of anecdotal and statistical data to share with other parents.

Developing a Parent Response Plan

Leadership team members and others, including parents who support single-sex instruction in your school, should work together to develop a parent-response plan. It is important to pull together information to support single-sex instruction as an option in your school and to address concerns when they arise. When needed, members of this group should be willing to make calls and do further research, especially when questions arise for which you do not have an immediate answer. Here are some of the concerns we have found expressed by parents:

- **Single-sex environments will not prepare boys and girls for personal relationships with one another**

As you work with parents on your leadership team and then in the community, be ready to point out that one of the primary benefits of the single-sex format is fostering the kind of confidence that will help students in their interpersonal relationships. It is a myth that single-sex environments harm boys and girls socially. In fact, the opposite is generally true—as boys and girls gain confidence in their same-sex classes, they become better at relating authentically to others, including persons of the opposite sex.

Furthermore, it is important to point out to parents who raise the socialization objection that in our society, our schools, our extracurricular activities, and our families, the genders have significant interactions. Indeed, there is no evidence from any country that single-sex environments harm socialization of boys and girls as working partners in the future workplace, in the family, or the community.

- **Single-sex classes are a form of gender discrimination—a mechanism to help the boys that will hurt the girls, or vice versa**

Be prepared to emphasize that neither gender has to lose for the other to win. What is important is that we work for all students by learning as much as we can about them, by teaching them in ways that show we understand how they learn, and by minimizing stress, distractions, and other impediments to learning. It is also important to note that though some political organizations, such as the ACLU, have objected to single-sex classes under the assumption that gender unfairness would ensue, they have been unable to provide proof of this result. In fact, a great deal of research, including our own, shows the opposite: when single-sex classes and programs are done carefully, they bring more parity to boys and girls, not less.

"Positive outcomes from single-sex education for both boys and girls include higher reading and foreign language achievement, less sex-stereotyped course taking patterns, more time spent on homework, higher educational aspirations, and decreased sex-role stereotyping. Positive effects are greatest among girls and among minority students of both sexes."

—National Association of State Boards of
Education policy update

Even with positive research to report, you may still run into visceral opposition. Gender and learning are volatile subjects. An illustration of the landscape in which you are now innovating is the basic disagreement among proponents of single-sex education about whether we should call classes of all girls or all boys "single-sex" or "single-gender." Even our terminology is in transition.

Keep in mind that parents, like all of us, are inextricably connected to personal experiences and ideas about what it means to be a man or a woman. Their opinions may therefore be based in large measure upon personal feelings, rather than upon information or arguments that they can readily articulate. Schools that are utilizing single-sex options are meeting parents' issues head on—by showing them evidence, such as you'll find in this book, that old stereotypical notions of gender are not being carried forward in today's single-sex classrooms.

And as you talk to parents about this, it can be crucial not to be so overwhelmingly in favor of single-sex education that you present it as the only good option. Most parents sense, even if they can't articulate it, that a lot of kids learn quite well in coed environments. Most people know that 99 percent of our schools are coed. Those of us who support single-sex options must always keep in mind that it is optional, and needs buy-in. It isn't something to force. If you readily acknowledge your awareness that there is no one model of education that is right for every student—some may do better in coed environments, but others may flourish in single-sex classes—parents are most likely to be open to this additional tool that you are bringing to your school as an opportunity for success and enrichment for their son or daughter.

"Those studies with the most positive affective outcomes from students took place in single-sex classes in which the students opted to participate. These students were more likely to 'admit' their enjoyment of these classes and more likely to take the opportunities provided to them to take advantage academically."

—Dr. Fran Spielhagen, *Debating Single-Sex Education*

Disseminating Parent Surveys and Gathering Resulting Information

Before going to the public to suggest single-sex options, make sure you have asked representative (or all) parents to complete a survey regarding interest. The following survey, or a modification of it, can be used by your school and community. It works well as a Word document sent via e-mail, but can also be handed out at community meetings in hard copy.

Once you've received the surveys back, take some time in your leadership team to pull out the data and any portable quotes from parents themselves that can be used to help you make your case to the public.

Parents Assess Single-Sex Arrangements (P.A.S.-S.A.)

#	Statement	Agree Strongly	Agree	Neutral	Disagree	Disagree Strongly
1.	I have been adequately informed about the option of single-sex classes for my children.					
2.	I have had experience with single-sex classes myself as a student.					
3.	I want my child to be in single-sex classes.					
4.	My spouse/partner agrees with my decision about single-sex classes.					
5.	My child agrees with the decision we made about single-sex class placement.					
6.	Single-sex classes help students learn better.					
7.	Single-sex classes provide a safer environment for children.					

(Continued)

Parents Assess Single-Sex Arrangements (P.A.S.-S.A.) *(Continued)*

#	Statement	Agree Strongly	Agree	Neutral	Disagree	Disagree Strongly
8.	I expect to see an improvement in my child's school achievement because of single-sex classes.					
9.	My child will probably enjoy single-sex classes.					
10.	Mixed classes create more social pressure than single-sex classes.					
11.	There will be more bullying in single-sex classes than in mixed classes.					
12.	Single-sex classes will allow my child to stay younger longer.					
13.	Mixed classes help children learn how to function in the real world.					
14.	I would encourage other parents to choose single-sex classes for their children.					
15.	Single-sex classes are a good option at this school.					

Source: ©P.A.S.-S.A., developed by F. R. Spielhagen, 2003. Used by permission.

WRAPPING UP THE MAIN POINTS

To set up a strong single-sex program it is important that you

- Identify the need and outline the challenges
- Review available research and investigate other successful programs

- Share the value of single-sex options with faculty—their buy-in is critical to the success of the program
- Work together on a leadership team to establish a vision and develop an action plan with desired outcomes
- Determine solutions to issues regarding more physical space, more teachers, scheduling, and so on
- Establish timelines for obtaining appropriate approval—principal, superintendent, board of education, board of trustees, and any other regulating authorities
- Communicate with stakeholders—students, parents, PTO, or PTA—and share research data, vision, and action plan
- Provide training for teachers and information sessions for parents
- Create a plan for implementation through collaboration and cooperation—follow and adapt it as you put the program into action

Four Tools for Evaluating Your Existing Single-Sex Instructional Program

I need survey tools that already work to evaluate my single-sex program. Where can I find these? I know there must be surveys in other schools that have worked. I don't want to re-invent the wheel.

—Elementary school principal

"Okay, we're doing it," a principal in Virginia told us. "We're now beginning our second year of single-sex classes. Most parents love what we're doing, some people don't, but in general, we're seeing good results. The question we have now is—what next? How do we keep getting better? How do we keep this going and help it grow organically into something even more successful?"

In Chapter Three, we provided you with analysis and tools to help you set up your single-sex program successfully. In this chapter, we'll assume you have had your program in place for several months—long enough to begin gathering some results data. Such data can be crucial to the continued success of your single-sex program, and so, we will devote the following pages to sharing several surveys for collecting data from students and parents. We hope these will further assist you as you reflect on your progress and refine your program for maximum results. We have found these surveys to be invaluable tools for principals and teachers who hope to continue to improve their programs.

STUDENT SURVEYS YOU CAN USE AS YOU EVALUATE YOUR PROGRAM

The following surveys are examples that can be used to obtain valuable feedback from students in your single-sex program. Each school will need to adapt the questions to match the specific needs of its program and the age and reading comprehension level of the students being surveyed. (Both of the student surveys for grades 5–7 rank a 4.4 grade level on the Flesch-Kincaid Readability Scale. The survey samples for grade levels 8–12 rank a 7.3 grade level.)

A PARENT SURVEY YOU CAN USE TO EVALUATE YOUR SINGLE-SEX PROGRAM

Parent surveys are crucial to the process of maintaining your program. This sample survey for parents ranks a 6.6 grade level on the Flesch-Kincaid Readability Scale. Reading level is an important consideration when asking for parent responses, and this sample takes into account diverse literacy levels.

These surveys can be replicated for your use, and we have waived copyright. However, we would love you to e-mail your disaggregated results, as appropriate, to info@gurianinstitute.com. We hope to be able to share your success with others so that they can learn from the pitfalls you have faced.

Student Survey for Boys (Grades 5–7)

1. Which do you like best, learning in a **class of all boys** or in a **class with both boys and girls**?

   Circle one: Class with all boys   Class with both boys and girls

2. Is it easier to concentrate in a **class of all boys** or in a **class with both boys and girls**?

   Circle one: Class with all boys   Class with both boys and girls

   Why? _____

   _____

3. For each of the following questions, circle one of these answers: Yes Maybe or No

   a) Now that you are in a class of just boys, do you feel more confident in **writing**?

   Yes   Maybe   No

   b) Now that you are in a class of just boys, do you feel more confident in **reading**?

   Yes   Maybe   No

   c) Now that you are in a class of just boys, do you feel more confident in **social studies**?

   Yes   Maybe   No

   d) Now that you are in a class of just boys, do you feel more confident in **math**?

   Yes   Maybe   No

   e) Now that you are in a class of just boys, do you feel more confident in **science**?

   Yes   Maybe   No

   f) Now that you are in a class of just boys, do you feel more confident **asking questions**?

   Yes   Maybe   No

   g) Now that you are in a class of just boys, do you feel more confident **answering questions?**

   Yes   Maybe   No

   h) Now that you are in a class of just boys, do you feel like **you have more friends**?

   Yes   Maybe   No

4. Information about you:

   Your grade in school: _____

   Your teacher's name: _____

   Today's date: _____

Thak you for participating in this survey.

Student Survey for Girls (Grades 5–7)

1. Which do you like best, learning in a **class of all girls** or in a **class with both boys and girls**?

   Circle one: Class with all girls   Class with both boys and girls

2. Is it easier to concentrate in a **class of all girls** or in a **class with both boys and girls**?

   Circle one: Class with all girls   Class with both boys and girls

   Why? _____

   _____

3. For each of the following questions, circle one of these answers: Yes Maybe or No

   a) Now that you are in a class of just girls, do you feel more confident in **writing**?

   Yes   Maybe   No

   b) Now that you are in a class of just girls, do you feel more confident in **reading**?

   Yes   Maybe   No

   c) Now that you are in a class of just girls, do you feel more confident in **social studies**?

   Yes   Maybe   No

   d) Now that you are in a class of just girls, do you feel more confident in **math**?

   Yes   Maybe   No

   e) Now that you are in a class of just girls, do you feel more confident in **science**?

   Yes   Maybe   No

   f) Now that you are in a class of just girls, do you feel more confident **asking questions**?

   Yes   Maybe   No

   g) Now that you are in a class of just girls, do you feel more confident **answering questions?**

   Yes   Maybe   No

   h) Now that you are in a class of just girls, do you feel like **you have more friends**?

   Yes   Maybe   No

4. Information about you:

   Your grade in school: _____

   Your teacher's name: _____

   Today's date: _____

Thak you for participating in this survey.

Student Survey (Grades 8–12)

1. Do you feel more comfortable in **single-sex or coed classes**?

   Circle one: Single-sex classes   Coed classes

   Why?_____

   _____

2. Circle the number which best describes your **level of confidence** in the following areas while you were **in coed classes**:

	Lowest Confidence				Highest Confidence
Writing	1	2	3	4	5
Reading (understanding what you read)	1	2	3	4	5
Social Studies	1	2	3	4	5
Math	1	2	3	4	5
Science	1	2	3	4	5
Technology	1	2	3	4	5
Class participation	1	2	3	4	5

3. Circle the number which best describes your **level of confidence** in the following areas while you were **in single-sex classes**:

	Lowest Confidence				Highest Confidence
Writing	1	2	3	4	5
Reading (understanding what you read)	1	2	3	4	5
Social Studies	1	2	3	4	5
Math	1	2	3	4	5
Science	1	2	3	4	5
Technology	1	2	3	4	5
Class participation	1	2	3	4	5

4. Check the box that best describes how **challenging** your single-sex classes have been in the following areas:

	Not Challenging Enough	Just Right	Too Challenging
Writing			
Reading			
Social Studies			
Math			
Science			
Technology			

5. Circle the number which best describes how **successful** you feel in your single-sex classroom in these areas:

	Low Success				High Success
Asking the right questions	1	2	3	4	5
Participating in classroom discussions	1	2	3	4	5
Learning information that will help me in the future	1	2	3	4	5
Making grades I'm proud of	1	2	3	4	5
Getting a fair and appropriate amount of attention in class	1	2	3	4	5
Getting along with classmates	1	2	3	4	5
Feeling accepted by peers	1	2	3	4	5
Behaving appropriately at school	1	2	3	4	5

6. In which classes do you usually feel **more successful**? Circle: Single-sex Coed

Why?_____

_____

_____

_____

7. Circle the number which best describes how successful you feel in your single-sex classroom in these areas:

	Low Enjoyment				High Enjoyment
Being at school	1	2	3	4	5
Spending time with classmates	1	2	3	4	5
Participating in class	1	2	3	4	5
Interacting with teachers	1	2	3	4	5
Learning	1	2	3	4	5
Writing	1	2	3	4	5
Reading	1	2	3	4	5
Social Studies	1	2	3	4	5
Math	1	2	3	4	5
Science	1	2	3	4	5

8. Do single-sex classes make learning easier or better in any ways?
   Circle one: Yes   No   If yes, list some of the ways:

   _____

   _____

9. Do single-sex classes make learning more difficult or worse in any ways?
   Circle one: Yes   No   If yes, list some of the ways:

   _____

   _____

10. Do you prefer single-sex classes or coed classes? Circle: Single-sex   Coed
    Why? _____

    _____

   Information about the person completing this survey:

   Circle one: Boy   Girl

   Date you completed this form: _____

   Thank you for your participation in this survey.

Parent Survey: Single-Sex Program

1. Check the box that best describes how **challenging** single-sex classes have been for your child in the following areas:

	Not Challenging Enough	Just Right	Too Challenging
Writing			
Reading			
Social Studies			
Math			
Science			
Technology			

2. Check the box that best describes how **successful** single-sex classes have been for your child in the following areas:

	Unsuccessful	Appropriately Successful	Very Successful
Writing			
Reading			
Social Studies			
Math			
Science			
Technology			

3. Check the box that best describes **confidence** level in the following single-sex areas of study:

	My Child Is Not Confident	My Child Is Confident	My Child Is Very Confident
Writing			
Reading			
Social Studies			
Math			
Science			
Technology			

4. Do you believe your child **concentrates** better in single-sex classes or in coed classes?

   Circle one: In single-sex classes   In coed classes

   Why?_____

   _____

5. Do you believe your child **learns better** in single-sex classes or in coed classes?

   Circle one: In single-sex classes   In coed classes

   Why?_____

   _____

6. Do you believe your child **feels less stress** in single-sex classes or in coed classes?

   Circle one: In single-sex classes   In coed classes

   Why?_____

   _____

7. Circle the number which best describes how much you believe your child has **enjoyed** participating in single-sex classes:

Lowest Enjoyment				Highest Enjoyment
1	2	3	4	5

8. What factors have contributed most to your child's **success** this year?

   _____

   _____

9. What factors have made school **challenging** for your child this year?

   _____

   _____

10. What skills do you think your child is **learning** in single-sex classes this year that will help him/her be more successful in the future?

   _____

   _____

11. Please feel free to share **any other information** regarding your child's experience in single-sex instruction this year.

   _____

   _____

Information regarding your child: Circle one: Boy   Girl

Child's grade level: _____ Child's teacher: _____ Date: _____

WRAPPING UP THE MAIN POINTS

As you move forward in your single-sex program, check out this short list of success steps. Keep them in mind, and include them on your meeting agendas as you utilize surveys to gather data. Carry them forward into the next chapters of this book. They can constantly help refocus your energies and dialogues as you share data in your community, and move forward.

- Reflect and refine—create an ongoing review process which includes:
  - personal feedback from teachers, students, and parents
  - results from data surveys and anecdotal reports
- Design strategies to overcome challenges (see the next chapters for help with this)
- Continue professional development through discussions, presentations, and trainings
- Use your best instincts to enhance communications and relationships with parents, teachers, and students by
  - building ever stronger bonds between home and school
  - helping students in the single-sex environment to develop stronger bonds with one another
  - celebrating students in this unique educational setting, creating a greater sense of unity
  - providing teachers with processing time they need to keep growing as teachers in single-sex environments

PART THREE

Teaching to the Learning Strengths of Boys and Girls

Here's what we found when we [went single-sex schoolwide]. Kids really became kids. The girls participated in physical education like they had never participated before. When we split those classes, participation shot up. The name-calling, the social behavior completely changed. The focus on academics went way, way up. . . . The parents in this school have finally got some peace of mind about their kids' academic wherewithal. They know that they're learning.

So what I'm telling you about single-sex education today, I guess, is—I am not the researcher, I am not the legal beaver, but I'm telling you I'm the practitioner and I'll tell you it works! It not only works in my opinion, it is the only way to fly in America right now when we have so many kids that are not making it.

—Benjamin Wright, 2003 Principal of the Year for Washington State and author of *Yes We Can If We Choose*

A Boy-Friendly Classroom—What Does It Look Like?

We don't like to be compared to the girls' classes. Sometimes teachers do that. Sometimes we ask them to make comparisons. I don't know why we do that, because we don't like to be compared. I guess we are hoping we did better than the girls did!

—Carl, middle school boy

Many boys are struggling in today's schools, and many find learning improvement in boys-only classrooms. With training and preparation under their belt, these boys' teachers instinctively and specifically end up creating (and constantly adapting toward) what we call the "boy-friendly" classroom. In our workbooks, *Strategies for Teaching Boys and Girls: Elementary Level* and *Strategies for Teaching Boys and Girls: Secondary Level,* we have detailed how to create a boy-friendly classroom in a coed environment. In this book, and in this chapter, we hope you'll find tools you can use to augment your own instincts on creating a boys-only, boy-friendly classroom. There is nothing quite like it!

A middle school teacher told us: "The single-sex classroom is an opportunity to help boys develop skills to meet their diverse challenges regarding motivation to learn; to enhance their varying strengths, and to improve their performance and their attitudes about school and learning. After all, what could be more fun than teaching a group of boys who are actively engaged in learning and doing? Their energy is contagious and they love those occasions when they get to fully engage in challenging activities, using their hands and bodies to become more productive learners."

So true!

TRY THIS: Tips for Teaching Groups of Boys

As you consider making all-boy classrooms places that maximize learning experiences for boys, consider these overarching goals:

- Recognize the diversity among boys and value their worth and their contributions
- Understand and meet the particular needs of boys
- Fully equip boys with skills and provide opportunities for boys to learn by doing
- Help boys explore new opportunities and recognize their accomplishments
- Emphasize problem solving and learning by doing
- De-emphasize talking when the boys' eyes glaze over
- Emphasize reading and writing that interest boys
- Validate boys' points of view and understand that boys have strong emotions too
- Help boys clear up stereotypes that limit their growth and stifle their creativity
- Build boys' confidence by using rather than stifling "boy energy"

TEACHING WITH AN UNDERSTANDING OF BOY ENERGY

Peggy Daniels recalls a particular Christmas morning when she and her teenage daughter, Rachel, were overwhelmed with boy energy in their lives. After years of avoiding the purchase of toy guns for their son Sam, Peggy and her husband, Rick, had finally allowed Santa to deliver two NERF guns with rotating barrels that noisily discharged five soft arrows in a row. Peggy and Rachel did not expect the boy energy she would witness as Rick and Sam enjoyed game after game of chasing each other upstairs and downstairs throughout the house, pounding each other with NERF arrows. Peggy recalls, "It was pure bedlam—a Christmas morning like no other." The whirlwind of activity went on and on for the rest of the day and through the remainder of the holiday.

Now, fifteen years later, she and Rachel still shake their heads and laugh when they think of that incredible display of boy energy, a kind of energy that, once directed and harnessed, can be used for immense successes in learning and growth.

Strategies Implemented at Boys' Latin School

Boys' Latin School in Baltimore, Maryland, has been educating boys in single-sex classes, kindergarten through twelfth grade, since 1844. With all that experience and expertise, the school still makes a consistent commitment to maintaining a current knowledge base including all the recent, exciting information about how boys learn. When we asked Stephanie McKew, the lower school learning specialist at Boys' Latin, to share some of the innovative things that were happening on campus to provide the best environment for boys, she gathered some excellent input from her colleagues, including:

- All divisions send home individualized monthly newsletters.
- The ESS department has included a "brain fact" and how it pertains to boys and learning in weekly e-news publications that are sent to the entire BL community, including alumni and parents.
- A consultant was hired to give eight lectures to parents on the theme "It's All About the Brain."

- All teachers have been given brain break strategies and activities to use during class periods. Faculty has been taught brain breaks throughout the school year at weekly faculty meetings. Each lower school and middle school staff member was given brain breaks typed and laminated on index cards so they are readily accessible while teachers are developing lessons.

- Teachers have been asked to list the class period objectives and agenda on the board each day so boys have a sense of timing and purpose for the lesson. Teachers have been encouraged to list classroom "procedures" rather than "rules."

- The upper school learning specialist includes a "Feature Teacher" presentation during upper school faculty meetings to highlight a teacher successfully using a male brain learning strategy (copies available). This presentation encourages and models teaching strategies already being implemented.

- Each learning specialist has taught students lessons focused on the brain and learning. The intent of these lessons has been to increase individual awareness and understanding of the brain and encourage metacognition and conscious decision making.

- Midterm exams were moved to before the winter break.

- Water was made readily available throughout all divisions. "Hydration stations" (coolers with cups) were set up in the middle school, and upper school students were able to carry water bottles. Lower school has water fountains, and boys were encouraged to get drinks anytime during the day.

- Recess has been reinstituted in the middle school.

- Technology is integrated throughout the school: Internet sites, Moodle, copies of notes, online test taking, and video clips enhance boys' ability to attend to information. Most teachers have laptops and ceiling-mounted projectors for technology use. Teachers display Internet sites, maps, graphs, as well the journal tool for writing on the tablet screen. Lower school also has an Elmo on each floor to project single-copy materials.

- The school has purchased bulbs that give off more "natural light" to replace current bulbs as they burn out.

- Stress balls (brains) were ordered and distributed to teachers in all divisions. In addition to stress balls, the lower school has also used Play-Doh® and Silly Putty® for some boys with greater attentional or sensory concerns.

- Standing desks are currently being piloted. A lower school father has extended the legs on several classroom desks as prototypes. The school is currently looking into designing its own standing desks. It has had positive results with the five standing desks piloted so far.

- Increased use of male mentoring between upper school and lower school boys.

Stephanie explained:

> At the beginning of the 2007–2008 school year, a colleague, Elizabeth, and I team taught all the boys in grades 1–5, a total of ten classes, a lesson covering the brain and learning. We projected pictures of the brain—the whole brain, dendrites and synapses—as well as diagrams that explain the components of learning, mind, body, and spirit, and the learning hierarchy. The importance of water, keeping the brain hydrated, and nutrition were also discussed. I specifically talked about the male brain, sharing information we had learned about the biological differences between the male and female brain at a developmentally appropriate level.
>
> The boys absolutely LOVED this. The discussion included explanation regarding learning and movement. **The boys were thrilled that the school understands this.** The boys were then taught three brain breaks, and it was explained to them how their teachers were going to use brain breaks this year.

The strategies being incorporated on the campus at Boys' Latin can be implemented at any school, public or private. These strategies can be used schoolwide and will help students in both single-sex and coed classes. Even piloting one or two of these strategies can make a big difference in performance, behavior, and attitude about being at school.

Understanding Boy Energy

In *The Minds of Boys,* we shared with readers that the minds of boys are "carried as much in their bodies as in their heads." Boys' Latin School understands this well. Boys' spatial brains are energized by objects moving through space (NERF arrows, footballs, rockets). Their bodies require movement, and from an early age most boys begin to actively practice being rough-and-tumble and active in their boy worlds. Most boys, even the most verbal boys who enjoy reading and writing, strive to be physically engaged with their world. They love to bang, touch, poke, push, shove, hammer, and explore.

Fortunately, the time has come in our culture when we can deeply understand this boy energy. Findings in brain research show us these classic boy behaviors are not just socialized, but also an expression of male brain biology and chemistry. The testosterone that bathed the male fetus during gestation promotes and affects the thinking and actions of boys, with the result that most boys, in varying degrees, prefer doing to processing, and building to written busywork. Most boys are more active learners than we may have realized before. They must engage their hands and bodies in order to engage their minds.

Because of their activity level, many boys need space to think, move, and position their materials for learning. Undisciplined behavior can easily occur when

boys feel cramped in a small space. Given the opportunity, boys tend to spread out across the room, using as much area as they can. If it is possible for each boy to have a table to himself, there is little doubt that most will choose this option. Many girls seem to prefer a more intimate classroom environment where they can sit close together, but sitting close is not easy for most boys.

As you work to build and maintain a boy-friendly classroom, you will be challenged to direct boy energy, and you'll intuitively turn that energy into productivity. Among the primary things you'll discover—something upon which many of your innovations will be connected—is the way boys use space and how they like to move around when doing their tasks.

TRY THIS: Use Humor When You Can

Middle school math and science teacher Kevin McManus told us:

"In my single-sex class, I have learned to be 'coach-like' with boys—to motivate them with challenges and humor."

From a very early age, boys employ humor to relate to one another. They love to make each other laugh and even to make their teachers laugh. A sense of humor is important to develop and encourage in boys, as it helps them to build friendships and better deal with their world. Their humor is everywhere and should also be a part of the classroom, for it is often the best reflection of their energy, and is a great bonding mechanism. When boys bond and form a team, they can accomplish just about anything.

Haisha, an attorney in Florida and mother of one son, told us this story:

> Just a couple of years ago, Jeffrey was a sixth grader who had struggled for years with learning disorders, dyslexia and attention-deficit disorder. Throughout his years in school, his fidgety boy energy was a distraction for his teachers and his classmates. Medication helped to some extent, but the side effects were a great concern to Jeffrey's physician and to us, his parents. Jeffrey fell further behind as he struggled to make the classroom work for him. Educational testing supported our belief that he was a very bright young man, but school was nevertheless a poor fit for him.

Relief for Jeffrey came when he entered middle school. We opted him into Ms. Jameson's boy-only sixth-grade classroom. Now his classmates were sixteen other boys. For Jeffrey, these boys, and Ms. Jameson's understanding of boy energy were life-changing.

As we talked to Haisha and learned more about this class, we learned that Ms. Jameson was excited to be teaching a class of all boys. An experienced teacher recently trained to teach in a single-sex classroom, she was aware of the challenges of a single-sex boys' classroom. It was her desire to make her classroom a boy-friendly setting where learning could be maximized. She had raised three sons and loved boy energy!

From Ms. Jameson we learned that for the first several weeks of the year, Jeffrey struggled to stay on task. Then one day Ms. Jameson noticed something different about him. Jeffrey's group was busy with an assigned project, and they had chosen a place on the floor in the corner of the room to spread out their materials and work. As Jeffrey lay on the floor on his belly, he was staying focused, contributing ideas, and being a productive member of his group. After class, Ms. Jameson mentioned this to Jeffrey, and he agreed that it was easier for him to work on the floor on his stomach. It helped him to control his fidgety behavior.

To Ms. Jameson this seemed like a simple thing, so from that point on he was allowed to make the floor his space for learning. It worked for Jeffrey and it worked for the class. He understood that at times he would need to return to his desk, but he became a happier, far more productive student, better able to manage his

learning because together they had found a better way to manage his behavior.

Traditionally, educators and parents would probably regard a student lying on the floor during class as inappropriate, or even disrespectful. Given Jeffrey's past struggles, however, Ms. Jameson was happy to use a boy-friendly strategy that would help him become more engaged in learning. She let him lie on his stomach and his performance improved. Other boys were allowed to use this technique and it helped them, too.

Another teacher, Crystal Fowler, who teaches single-sex math classes for both eighth-grade boys and girls, has also noticed the importance of "physical learning" and physical movement for boys. Crystal says, "My female students sit quietly, listen to directions and stay in their seats, whereas the male students like to talk more and move around the room. If you came into my female class you would see girls sitting in their seats working on a lesson, but in the male classroom you will see boys scattered around the room—some on bean bags, others on rugs, and others sitting against the walls working on their assignments. They spread out around the room to find comfortable spots to complete their assignments."

Crystal also notices that transition time is different in the male classroom. The female students move easily from one topic to another, but the males find this difficult. When boys are asked to move to another activity, and the transition is not well planned, they will begin talking and get off task. Crystal uses a "read aloud" to help make the transition smoother. She has found that the boys will settle down and accept change more easily if she reads to them for a few minutes between topics, letting them move around responsibly while she reads.

The Advantages of Movement to the Learning Brain

"I hate being still . . . I've always got to be moving. I've always got to be challenged."

—Tiger Woods

Movement is an essential part of life. It helps us take in air to breathe, helps us eat and digest our food, keeps us alert, and awakens our minds to new information. It allows us to express ourselves in so many ways and actually brings our world into our minds. We are learning more and more about just how important movement is to the learning process for boys and girls, men and women.

In her book, *Smart Moves,* biologist, educator, and author Carla Hannaford tells us that there must often be movement of the body for the brain "to pin down a thought." Even simple movements like those involved in writing and talking are essential to help our brains make sense of information. She also explains that although thinking can certainly happen while we sit still, movement often has to accompany the thought process if we are to make neural connections to truly anchor our thoughts into memory.

When teachers at Summit School in Winston-Salem, North Carolina, learned how important it is for boys to have movement, they realized that boys would benefit from simply having the opportunity to stand up in the classroom. The teachers

solicited the help of their maintenance department to build a few tabletop podiums for the boys. Some of the boys use this option a lot. It allows them to stand and more comfortably continue to participate and do their assignments.

Another easy and productive way to get boys out of their seats and moving is to have them do a **pair-share** activity. Have boys walk with a partner for two minutes, each boy sharing some aspect of what has been discussed in class—what they remember, what had the most meaning to them, how they will use the information, what surprised them. These physical movements, walking and talking, will facilitate the brain's understanding, storage, and memory process. It will also allow students to learn more from each other and see how others may have interpreted the same information differently.

If you pay close attention to the state of boys during the school day, you will notice that some may seem to "zone out" in the classroom, especially when a teacher has been talking for more than ten or fifteen minutes. The male brain goes into a "rest state," and when their brains go into this state, boys simply cannot be successful learners. When you notice a boy beginning to fidget, tapping a pencil, poking a classmate from behind, or trying to move in any number of ways, these are signals that his attention is wandering and he is in need of physical movement to reenergize his mind for learning.

"I seldom attend a faculty meeting without noticing how difficult it is for some teachers to sit still. Several will seek opportunities to get up from their chairs and stand in the back of the room for a few minutes. As a high school teacher, I do understand that it is important to help students, especially college-bound students, learn that there are times when they will need to remain seated and do their best to listen and take notes. But I do not believe that students should have to sit for long periods of time, especially for forty-five to fifty minutes every period, every day. A lecture for more than twenty to twenty-five minutes is so painful for boys and some girls too."

—John Zazzaro, Carolina Day

Teachers who struggle with the idea of providing movement opportunities in their classroom should at least allow the most restless students to get up. This is easy to accomplish by having them help out more often in the classroom by passing out materials, taking up assignments, or pairing up or grouping to review information. Just a little movement can help these students reengage or calm their restless behavior in order to get back on task.

The Importance of Recess and Physical Education

"Exercise is the magic bullet for creating mental energy. The immediate effect of exercise is increased energy, so tactically it can be used at any point of a flagging day to get you up and going."

—Dr. Robert Arnot, *The Biology of Success*

When we exercise, our intent is usually to improve our physical well-being—to firm up muscles, improve cardiovascular strength, and shed a few pounds. But one of the most important benefits of exercise is the way it affects our brains. It makes us more alert and can decrease stress and improve our mood.

As schools work to meet accountability goals, they often feel that time allotted for PE and recess is time taken away from learning the core curriculum—the information needed for the test. However, if we agree that boys are falling behind in school and that they need more opportunities to exercise their bodies and energize their minds, then we understand the importance of PE and recess. Much of the movement and physical activity vital to the brains and bodies of boys and girls is currently missing in school. This is a contributing factor to the struggles that our boys face.

In addition, PE and recess provide opportunities for free play. In these situations, students have the opportunity to

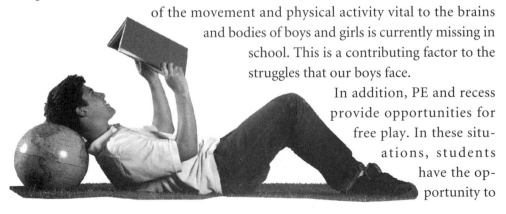

practice getting along and working out problems that arise while playing with others. A report from the American Academy of Pediatrics released in October 2006 suggests that "recess can foster creativity and social skills," and argues that "when play is undirected, kids become resourceful in figuring out conflict resolution, negotiation and even leadership—which might not surface as naturally in an adult-structured atmosphere, when children are more likely to 'acquiesce to adult rules and concerns.'"

MOVEMENT ACTIVITIES YOU CAN USE IN YOUR CLASSROOM RIGHT NOW

"Today, it seems, we are finally coming to grasp that movement and sensory experiences are the fertile soil for continual brain development and growth in a lifetime—and that these experiences actually cause the brain to constantly transform itself in unimaginably plastic ways."

—Carla Hannaford

Here are some activities for adding movement and creating energy in your single-sex classroom. Remember that although boys may need it more, girls need it too. So do teachers! Be sure to get up and moving along with your students.

Brain Gym® activities are designed to energize and motivate students, to help with balance and coordination, and to change the mental state of students, promoting greater potential for learning. These activities can be used to stimulate the brain for specific academic and behavioral improvement. Different Brain Gym exercises help with reading skills and reading comprehension, thinking and organization, spelling, math, eye-hand coordination for writing, listening, speaking, self-awareness, and so forth. Brain Gym is a quick, effective way to help connect the two hemispheres of the brain. Once students are familiar with these activities, they can be used whenever the class needs a quick break to refocus and reenergize. Most can be done with little time away from classroom instruction, and some options are specifically designed to help students prepare for writing, reading, concentration, and so on. The activities are easy to learn and there are several books that explain the movements with photographs. You can Google "Brain Gym" and find many resources. Popular Brain Gym and other mind-energizing exercises can be found in these resources:

Brain Gym by Paul E. Dennison and Gail E. Dennison

Smart Moves—Why Learning Is Not All in Your Head by Carla Hannaford

Hands On—How to Use Brain Gym in the Classroom by Isabel Cohen and Marcelle Goldsmith

Making the Brain Body Connection by Sharon Promislow

Learning With the Body in Mind by Eric Jensen

"In addition to less lecture and reading and more hands-on activity and group work, we do daily 'brain breaks.' One is the basic Brain Gym. I try to find some time each day to get their hearts pump-ing—this can be done in the classroom with some jumping jacks, cross-overs or any number of Brain Gym activities."

—Dave Curtis, 5th grade teacher

Here are some examples of Brain Gym activities you can put to use right now. (*Note:* The following is used with permission of Edu-Kinesthetics, Inc.)

Brain Buttons

The brain buttons are just above the area where the carotid arteries branch, bringing freshly oxygenated blood to the brain. To do this activity, first place one hand over the navel. This will bring attention to the center of the body and the core muscles that help with balance. With the opposite hand, spread the index finger and the thumb. Then use these to massage the indentations (brain buttons) directly under the collar bone to the right and left of the sternum. This stimulates a fresh supply of oxygen to the brain to keep you more alert, and this activity can be done while standing or seated.

Cross Crawls

This movement is basically a cross-lateral walking in place, and its several variations involve moving one arm and an opposite leg while crossing the mid-line of the body. While standing, slowly touch the right elbow to the raised left knee and then the left elbow to the raised right knee, and repeat this for approximately one minute. This activates both sides of the body and both sides of the brain simultaneously, and helps stimulate the growth of nerve cells in the corpus callosum, thus improving communication between the two hemispheres and therefore the ability to think and reason.

Hook-Ups

While standing, cross one ankle over the other. Extend arms in front of you with the backs of your hands together and thumbs facing down. Now lift one hand over the other with palms facing and interlock your fingers. Roll the locked hands down and then in toward your chest, keeping the elbows down and shoulders relaxed. Now rest your tongue on the roof of your mouth. Hold this position for a minute or so. Then start again, this time crossing the opposite ankle over the other. This activity stimulates both hemispheres of the brain, assists with motor coordination, and helps quiet and calm students so they can refocus and improve learning and memory. It is great to use this activity prior to having a discussion with a young student who is in trouble or upset.

Energy Yawns

This is one of the most frequently used Brain Gym activities because it activates so many areas for learning. For example, when a child is tense from reading, the jaw tightens and nerve function in that area decreases. When that occurs, the child's eyes do not work as well together. The Energy Yawn helps to relax those muscles and thereby improves nerve function to the eyes, facial muscles, and mouth. To do this, simply massage the temporomandibular joint (TMJ) areas right in front of the

ears where the lower and upper jaw meet. Now, while continuing to massage the TMJ area, take a deep yawn, expanding your diaphragm and exhaling completely. Repeat the Energy Yawn several times. This adds fresh oxygen to energize the brain and removes some of the excess carbon dioxide. Energy Yawning is a great way to help detoxify the system, manage good vision, and relax the body.

Move! Move! Move!

Here are activities created by teachers like you. These can be used whenever necessary, and right now!

- **Toss a soft ball** to the person who will ask or answer the next question or perform the next task. Not only is the movement great, so is the spatial component and the eye-hand coordination.

- Consider allowing students to hold **squeeze balls** while seated for listening activities in class. This gives the fidgety student something to do with his or her hands—and works well if the kids agree to use the squeeze balls only to help them stay alert and focused. Boys who have trouble focusing during writing assignments can be helped by squeezing the squeeze ball in their non-writing hand. For many boys, even this small amount of movement can help them stay more engaged during written work.

- **Everyone gets up** to turn in papers or pick up supplies. Though many teachers prefer to keep a majority of kids in their seats when collecting homework or other assignments, consider allowing all students to bring their papers to the front of the classroom or pick up their own supplies from designated areas around the room. This allows all kids to get up and move. Teachers with good classroom management skills can train students to make this happen quickly and with little confusion.

- Have students stand up and practice their spelling words by using their finger to **write the words on the back of a partner**. Let the partner guess the words.

- Have students stand up and ask a student to **create a movement pattern** for the class to perform. Repeat several times. Then ask another student to add to the pattern or create a different pattern. For example:

  First student: stomp, jump, snap, clap

  Second student: snap, snap, jump, jump

  Then put it all together: stomp, jump, snap, clap, snap, snap, jump, jump

- **Just stand up!** Students can stand and listen for a few moments, then sit down again to continue. Add a stretch or some calisthenics for more movement.

- **Employ music.** Remember that movement and music go hand in hand. Use lively music when students are cleaning up or transitioning to another activity. They will move more quickly and accomplish more in a shorter period of time. Energetic music will really get students moving—they will naturally tap their feet or snap their fingers. Scientists say that music seems to involve the brain at almost every level.

If you teach older students—teenagers—you may think they won't enjoy these movement activities. Actually, most do enjoy them, though for some they take a little getting used to. If nothing else, all teenagers enjoy just standing up and stretching. The adolescent brain needs movement and novelty to stay actively engaged in learning, and though you may feel that you need to stay focused on content at all times, without an occasional brain break, time spent on content may be wasted. Once students are familiar with a few of these activities, teachers find it possible to have students stand up and participate (such as the

Hook-Ups Brain Gym activity) without causing a break in a class discussion. Teachers who enjoy movement activities and recognize the benefits will be able to successfully convince older students of their value. Just a minute of standing and moving can make a big difference for some students. Employing movement is an instructional strategy that works. Have fun with it, and so will your students!

"We move around a lot! Desks are arranged in rows, but we do a lot of partner and small group work, so each time we move into a 'team' we have to move to a new spot. That helps calm some of the restlessness from sitting in a desk all day. I also allow boys who are having trouble staying awake or sitting still during direct instruction to move to a new seat or stand up as long as they are not disrupting anyone else. One of the favorite games of the boys in my class is 'Musical Drills.' Students line up and march or walk around the room as long as music is playing. When the music stops, whoever is at the designated spot has to answer a flashcard or other basic skills question. This is extremely effective after lunch and recess for getting settled back into learning mode."

—Heather Calvert, Ewing Middle School teacher

USING SPACE IN BOY-FRIENDLY WAYS

Peggy heard an interesting story from a teacher while facilitating training in Florida's Broward County. It seems a boy in the teacher's coed class was frequently upsetting the girl who shared a table with him in class. Whenever she got up from the table, he would push her books and materials over to the farthest end. Upon returning she would spread her things out again to work, only to have the same thing happen the next time she moved away. On occasion the young man would push her things completely off the table onto the floor. Upset, she sought the teacher's help, and though the teacher intervened, the behavior did not stop. Finally, the teacher realized that the boy's actions were not caused by any animosity toward the girl, but by the sheer frustration of having to share a space with someone else. She moved him from the table to a single desk and the problem was solved.

An awareness of the need for movement coupled with an understanding of the use of physical space can matter a great deal in a boy-friendly classroom. Extra space in boys-only classes helps to eliminate distractions and improve focus. The opportunity to add distance between students at times means fewer opportunities for unnecessary physical contact. Thus a classroom arranged for more space for boys to work, build, and be active will also help to engage the spatial learning areas of the boys' brains.

Within Their Space—An Environment for Learning

Because vision is the best sensory mode for boys, we should provide boys with as much natural and bright light as possible. This makes a big difference in how boys perform and how they feel. Both boys and girls benefit from good lighting because it slows the body's production of melatonin, which causes drowsiness, but it is especially helpful for most boys because they are so dependent on vision to learn.

DID YOU KNOW? THE LEARNING BRAIN NEEDS LIGHT!

Our bodies need at least 1,000 lux (one lux is equal to the illumination of a surface one meter away from a single candle) to reap the biological benefits of light. Lighting in most rooms, especially those that don't have windows to let in any natural light, have 600 lux at best. Get a light meter and measure the light available to you and your students in your classroom. Is it adequate? If not, talk to your administration about how to increase the levels.

Teachers who are creating boy-friendly classrooms know that boys need more visual and physical stimuli to help them retain what they learn. Visually, many boys (and some girls) prefer a room that is less cluttered and more organized. When it comes to covering wall space, teachers understand the value of posters and information that students can frequently reference for learning (charts, periodic tables, number lines). Some teachers notice that boys pay more attention to items that are placed on classroom walls than girls do. Girls are far more interested in making eye contact with other students and the teacher, while boys spend more time looking around the room, keeping their spatial-mechanical brains engaged. Paying attention to items that have been posted on the walls can be good—if you take the time to put up posters and charts, you hope they will be noticed. However, on a day-to-day basis, too many items on the walls can actually become distractions for many boys. Teachers should therefore frequently assess what they have displayed, keeping the items to which students regularly refer, removing older items, and adding information about what is currently being taught and discussed in the classroom.

Using Flexible Seating Options

Teachers who work with boys often employ flexible seating options. Seating arrangements should change frequently to add variety and a new perspective, and to provide settings that correspond with the types of learning activities that are taking place. For group discussions, if the goal is to get every student engaged in sharing ideas and opinions, placing boys in a circle is often the best option. When it is time for more individualized tasks such as writing or taking a test, row seating may help boys focus. When students must share a table, it is best not to put close friends together, or boys who do not seem to get along.

"An aspect of my classroom that has been a huge part of my students' success is providing them with flexible seating arrangements. Students have the option of sitting at tables, in desks, on stools at the science tables, in the literacy center (which has comfortable recliners), or in the revision center (which

has three more comfortable seats). This is a great way to motivate students and helps when we are transitioning into stations or small group activities."

————————————

—Anastasia, 6th grade teacher in the B.E.S.T. Academy
for Boys, Atlanta, Georgia

Using Tables

Tables are a good option for the all-boy classroom, as they can be moved into different configurations and provide more working space for collaborative efforts and hands-on activities. They can be pushed back and out of the way for occasions when students work on the floor or perform skits.

To accommodate all boys, especially boys like the one who could not share his space, the optimal situation would be a variety of seating: some desks, some tables, an easy chair, a rug area for working on the floor, even a couple of rocking chairs for boys who need to move while they listen or read.

If the room is small, these extra options may not be a possibility. Of course, teachers who include special seating options for boys need to be prepared for the competition that may arise and be ready to make decisions about who uses the favored seating, and when. Boys also need a room that will accommodate sitting in a circle with their teacher for discussion, a method that puts everyone on an equal footing, with each person's participation viewed as important.

Two Hidden Influences on Effective Learning

Like movement and exercise, which increase the flow of oxygen to the brain, water provides hydration, relieves stress, and is an essential element for our physical and mental well-being. Water makes up 70–80 percent of our body weight and approximately 90 percent of our brain. The electrical impulses that carry messages back and forth from our brain to our body require hydration to function properly. Clean drinking water is the best source of this hydration, as many beverages, especially those containing caffeine, contain diuretics which actually dehydrate our systems.

Boys in boy-friendly classrooms are often seen drinking plenty of water each day—this keeps their brains alert, removes waste and toxins from their systems,

improves concentration, and helps minimize stress. Teachers have learned that by the time a student feels thirsty he is already in the second stage of dehydration, at which point there is an increase in cortisol, the body's stress hormone. When cortisol levels go up, learning often goes down, so teachers should allow boys to drink water responsibly. Dehydration causes lethargy and mental slowdown, but within five minutes of consuming water, there is a marked improvement in learning as stress levels in the brain decrease.

Teachers who have learned the importance of water have also, quite often, factored in a second hidden stressor on the learning brains of boys: temperature. When the classroom temperature is too hot, there is a direct effect on the brain function and learning of all kids, especially boys. Researchers tell us that discomfort with room temperature will affect neurotransmitters in the brain, changing the mood of the learner and becoming an obstacle to learning, sometimes even promoting aggressive behavior. Most boys seem to work best in a classroom around sixty-nine degrees; girls often prefer a classroom that is about five degrees warmer.

Using the Outdoor Classroom with Boys

With increasingly busy schedules, people are spending more and more of their days indoors, enjoying less sunlight and less fresh air. Taking your class outdoors can provide boys with more space to move, clean air to breathe, and a rich sensory experience. Sunlight and fresh air help us to relieve stress, improve mood, and recharge our thinking. Without enough light, our brains send our bodies the message that it is time to be drowsy.

Taking students outdoors is a brain- and body-friendly activity that has the potential to be a rewarding experience.

Taking students outdoors is a brain- and body-friendly activity that has the potential to be a rewarding experience. Teachers will take students outside more often if they plan such classes with a purpose and involve students in establishing the procedures for outdoor experiences. Students can learn that the privilege of going outdoors is dependent on their behavior—that the freedom of going outside requires student responsibility and respectful participation in the learning activity.

Many indoor classroom activities work equally well outdoors. Students can learn math facts using sticks and pebbles; explore habitats; build and test projects, such as models of solar homes they have created for their unit on energy; collect leaves; use hopscotch to practice verb conjugations; explore stream ecology; have a discussion. It is also an opportunity for many teachable moments, such as the importance of caring for the environment.

Certainly students of all ages love the outdoor classroom experience, from prekindergarten through college. And why not end a great class outdoors with a five-minute game of slow-motion tag? Your students will have fun, and you will help them recharge for the next learning experience.

Making the Most of the Space You Have

It is wonderful to have a large classroom with room for learning centers, as well as open space for performance and movement. It is great to have the flexibility to

take students outdoors for learning. However, in the end, teachers have to deal with the classrooms to which they are assigned, and they must do their best to make their space into the best possible learning environment for the students and subject(s) they teach. All of the above conditions—space, seating, lighting, visual stimuli, classroom layout, and temperature—matter greatly; however, nothing plays a more important role than the teacher creating a warm, inviting atmosphere. To maximize learning for all students, boys should feel safe, accepted, valued, and comfortable in their classroom environments.

ENGAGING A BOY'S COMPETITIVE SPIRIT

"Another way the boys are coming together is when there is a schoolwide competition they really strive to win. From a food drive to drug awareness decorations, the boys really pull together and try to win. We have won or been top three in every competition."

—Michael Lofton, 8th grade single-sex class teacher

Most boys, and some girls, are naturally competitive. Providing opportunities for them to learn through competition is a great idea. Teachers can employ games for learning or for a review prior to a test. Competition not only engages students to learn, but also promotes spirit and motivation in the classroom.

Sometimes, especially with boys, the competition just surfaces on its own. Here is a telling example shared by Stephanie Howell, lower school librarian at Carolina Day School:

Knowing that boys are seldom interested in books with girls as protagonists, I decided to give separate book talks to the boys and girls in our fifth grade classes. The students thought this was a fine idea, especially because the group that I was not speaking with was allowed to

read in the picture book room by themselves. After a few minutes to look for books independently, the boys settled into the picture book room. The girls gathered in a semicircle on the carpet around me and began chattering about the books stacked nearby.

As I spoke about each book, the girls gave little squeals of excitement or interjected, "I want that one!" They asked me to tell them about the books I liked as a girl, and they wanted to know if I had read the book we were discussing, and if it was "good"? They were most excited about a book of personality quizzes. Every girl wanted to check out that one. They remained focused and attentive throughout the book talks and checked out many of the books I had offered.

During the next class, I reminded the girls that they would be reading in the picture book room while I had a book talk with the boys. I found the boys standing around one of the library tables looking at magazines and chatting. Remembering from our professional reading about gender differences that boys often prefer to stand and will listen without appearing to, I offered to let them stay where they were as long as they were quiet while I talked about some books. They grunted agreeably and continued flipping through their magazines. I talked about book after book, with exciting adventure, sports, blood and guts, a basketball team that practiced in their boxers, everything I could think of that they might like. From my perspective, the boys were completely unfazed—most not even glancing at the covers of the books as I held them up. I finished, offered to check out any of the books they wanted, and walked away thinking this had been a complete failure.

As soon as I left the table, the boys pounced on the books, sorted out the ones they wanted, and asked me to flip coins for groups of boys who wanted the same book. One such pair was Chase and Cedric who both wanted a DK NASCAR book. I flipped the coin and Cedric won. Then Chase said jovially, "Oh, I would have let Cedric have it even if I won. I have that book at home." I asked why he had bothered to have me flip the coin if he already owned the book. Chase looked straight at me and said, "To see if I could win!"

I ended up checking out just as many books to the boys as I had to the girls, even though the boys had given little indication that they were paying any attention to the book talks.

Several things come to mind after reading this narrative. One part of this story is the element of competition and just how much it means to the boys. What can teachers learn from the competitive drive of boys? First, we should enjoy it when we see it—after all, it is a sign of engagement. The fact that most boys love to play and to compete suggests that finding ways to employ competition in our classrooms will add productive energy and increase learning. Adding more game-oriented activities and competition not only enhances their learning, but also helps satisfy the desire of many boys to have more time to play.

"When my teacher adds activities that include teamwork or competition, it makes school a more interesting environment."

—Peter, 10th grade boy

Another interesting aspect of this story is that Stephanie allowed the boys to stand and continue looking at magazines, hoping they would nevertheless listen and be engaged in the book talk. As long as boys can commit to remaining quiet and not distracting others, they should at times be given this option. Would the same boys have been as cooperative and as engaged if they had been required to be seated, still, and quiet? Or would their energy and their need for movement have eventually caused them to become distractions? Perhaps their "boy code" prevented them from acting engaged in the same way that the girls did (seated, eyes on the reader, showing excitement for what was being shared, asking questions), but the boys certainly rushed to check out books. Mission accomplished!

A Few Warnings Regarding Competition

First, our youngest students (third grade and below) do not yet truly understand the concept of competition. It confuses them and can lead to unnecessary conflict, so it is usually best not to use classroom competition for this age group.

Second, although we employ competition to increase boy motivation, students may at times use their competitive spirit to make comparisons that are damaging. For example, if a boys' class asks how they did on a test or assignment in comparison to a girls' class, and we make the mistake of providing them with a disappointing answer, we run the risk of sending boys a different message than we intended. Remember that boys are great at keeping score. If the boys hear that the girls did better, the boys see it as "girls win, boys lose." Boys want to compete with any group they perceive as competing with them. If they lose, they feel that the teacher sees them as losers too. In the end the message boys receive is that they do not do as well on tests or they don't write as well, or even that the teacher likes girls better. The same holds true for girls in other areas (such as technology). So it is best not to make such comparisons or provide either group with information that might allow them to make comparisons that are damaging or potentially detrimental to their learning.

Finally, a good way to promote learning through competition, and to help boys and girls win and lose responsibly and respectfully, is to use team competition in the class between teams that are constantly changing members. Remember that when competition is employed, the teacher should always keep the end goal in mind, carefully planning for a win-win situation. The teacher's role is always that of coach, encouraging and complimenting students on what they know, and never making unnecessary comparisons.

Successful Teachers for Boys

We have already discussed a number of factors that are important for the learning environment of boys. None, however, is more important than the teacher. Successful teachers of boys understand their many characteristics and have a passion for helping boys feel comfortable and smart in their classrooms.

Dr. Gary Ross is the middle school principal at Stratford Academy in Macon, Georgia, and a former math teacher who has enjoyed his many experiences teaching single-sex math. He has a wealth of information regarding differences in teaching boys and girls and has presented at conferences on the topic. Dr. Ross believes "that a teacher's personality matters so much . . . and that teachers need to understand gender differences and apply best practices related to that understanding in their classrooms, whether coed or single gender." He says, "In boys' classes, teachers should be loud and also willing to allow boys to be loud."

TRY THIS: Be an Effective Boy Teacher

To be effective, follow your best instincts, and consider constantly refining these tools in your toolbox. Let's remember, though some men find it easier to relate to boys, and many boys respond better to a louder (often male) teacher voice, even a voice that is mildly confrontational, women can relate well to boys too, and boys need both male and female teachers. Women who relate best to boys usually have many boy stories to share with the boys they teach!

♂ Teach character and promote high expectations for academic performance and social maturity.

♂ Respectfully tell boys the truth, even about the hard things.

♂ Understand that boys are emotional too, and try to find time and appropriate ways to help them express their feelings in boy ways, ideally while walking together or doing a game or activity.

♂ Help boys wrestle with issues of anger management. Model good anger management, and tell the boys when they are stepping over the line. When necessary, provide discipline for their errors.

♂ Be "fair" in the eyes of boys. Help boys create and understand rules, and help all boys live by the rules.

♂ Don't take things personally, and know when to hold the authority (be the alpha) for boys.

♂ Guide boys to move beyond stereotypes and recognize the value of diversity in people and ideas. Boys need to develop a more inclusive sense of what it means to be male. When boys in an all-male classroom have the opportunity to discuss stereotypes and learn to value differences, then those boys who are not at the top of the pecking order will find school a more protected space for learning and discovering their own path.

♂ Share your life experiences, and even your mistakes, so that boys may say, "Well you know what I mean. You went through that too."

♂ Understand boy energy and boy humor; and tolerate more noise and more boy behavior at times. Be patient, flexible, and smart about boys.

♂ Create and employ opportunities for boys to move and to engage in active, hands-on learning.

♂ Explain directions more than once and in more than one way, being short and concise.

♂ Help boys find their spoken and written words through activities such as brainstorming and drawing.

♂ Engage boys in reading through such activities as bringing adult males into their classrooms to do book talks, to share experiences and expertise, and to serve as mentors.

OBSERVATIONS FROM TEACHERS OF BOYS

Teachers Bebe and John Zazzaro have twin boys and work in a boys' summer camp each year. They have some interesting perspectives to share about boys. Each insight is immensely useful to a single-sex classroom.

- Most boys do not enjoy or take much from lectures. In fact, they often resent lectures for instruction. While all students must learn to listen to people speak and be cooperative during times when this happens, few boys, especially young boys in elementary and middle school, can do this successfully for more than fifteen to twenty minutes.

- Those who struggle with boys often try to be too verbal with them, especially as they attempt to explain to a boy what he has done wrong. Typically, the boy will listen for a few minutes, but then his thoughts turn to: "This is too much talk. I will take my punishment. I just don't want to talk about it."

- Teachers should, at times, put themselves as equals with boys in the classroom. Stand up and deliver the lesson—hopefully a short one—then sit down on their level to talk about it. Sitting down signals to boys that it is now okay for them to talk equally with the teacher about what they are learning. It creates a more relaxed atmosphere for boy discussions.

- A teacher should figure out "where boys need to be," and then plant the seeds to help them get there. Being too direct sometimes just doesn't work. Remind boys in small ways on many occasions "where they need to be." For example, in a situation where a teacher is trying to make a point about a boy's need to improve a behavior, the teacher might say, "Remember Ben, you did this last week, and I told you then why it wasn't a good thing to do. This is just another example of the same thing." That's frequently enough to say to a boy.

- If a boy is in transition—a time when he is trying to decide which path to take, one path being less favorable—find opportunities through reading and discussion to address good choices versus bad choices.

WRAPPING UP THE MAIN POINTS

As mentioned earlier, many of the characteristics of a classroom that works well for boys will also work well for some girls. In fact, none of the strategies we recommend for boys will in any way hurt girls—so if you are still working in a coed classroom, use these strategies without worry!

- Employ movement activities
- Include adequate recess and PE
- Provide for regular hydration
- Adapt the learning environment for your class—boys, girls, or coed
- Take students outdoors to learn
- Include competition in the classroom

A Girl-Friendly Classroom—What Does It Look Like?

Sometimes I don't concentrate when I'm with boys because I kind of want them to notice me.

—Isabelle, 6th grade girl

Tameka Alexander is a literacy coach at the Coretta Scott King Young Women's Leadership Academy in Atlanta, Georgia. Visiting her classroom, it is evident that she gave a lot of thought to the environment she wanted to create.

Tameka told us,

> Classrooms can evoke many feelings. I wanted my classroom to make students feel a sense of safety, warmth, and coziness while being purposeful. Classroom rules are created by the students in the classroom as a community of learners. This helps to set the

115

expectation for behavior and communication that is acceptable for every member of the learning community. The use of real plants, strategic lighting, and inspirational signs throughout the classroom create warmth and coziness. Classroom supplies necessary for the daily functioning of learners are purposefully placed in areas that are easily accessible. My favorite aspect of the classroom is definitely the classroom mailbox! Students are free and encouraged to express their thoughts and feelings by writing a letter to me; then, flipping the sign hanging above the pink gift bag mailbox laced with ribbon boasts

"YOU HAVE MAIL" to indicate a letter has arrived! Students know they can expect a response soon that addresses their letter.

All of the planning, searching high and low, and strategic use of space are all worth it to hear a child's voice say, "Wow, look at the

room! I would love to learn in here!" Children who pass by will often float into the classroom with the common question, "Ms. Alexander, what happens in that tent?" This is when I know my job of creating the perfect girl-friendly space has been successful! This space will be one in which quiet conversations about text and life can take place; a space is transformed from a classroom into a "girl-friendly" environment!

As you make plans to set up single-sex girls' classrooms, you have the freedom to make those classrooms even more "girl friendly." Like Ms. Alexander, you can incorporate all that research has taught us about how girls learn best, and create a world that leads girls to greater levels of motivation, empowers them to take risks, and builds their confidence as learners in community.

You can also help girls through their encounters with the uncertain and confusing paths of young adulthood. A girl's growth into adolescence is sometimes marked by drops in self-esteem, which can cause her to underestimate what she can do in school and in life. As educators, we have the opportunity and the responsibility to guide, support, and encourage girls in ways that emphasize their worth and inspire them to greater heights. Girls need to be convinced that their words are heard and that they are valued as individuals who can excel in all areas. The messages we send girls fall on welcome ears when they express our unfaltering belief in them as powerful and competent individuals.

"One of my favorite teachers was my geography teacher because she never gave us notes from a textbook. Instead, she educated us on globalization by relating her own experiences and travels."

—Annie, 12th grade girl

"My chemistry teacher is very smart and he talks very enthusiastically about everything. He is so happy about chemistry that his enthusiasm is contagious and spreads to the students."

—Jessica, 10th grade girl

Single-sex instruction is an opportunity to create a more girl-friendly and girl-supportive environment, presenting subjects in ways that remove many of the stereotypical influences that negatively affect girls. When science is taught without the bias that favors boys, girls have an equal chance of discovering a passion for science. In single-sex classrooms, there exists the opportunity for girls to learn that they can become young scientists and mathematicians, that they can be the best in science, the best in math, and the best in technology. The single-sex classroom allows teachers to focus on celebrating what girls can do and what girls can become. Girls are then able to move more confidently into leadership roles that show them that they are individuals who can effect change. The support and guidance of teachers who understand girls and truly care about their progress are key to this quest.

TRY THIS: Strategies for Teachers in Single-Sex Girls' Classrooms

- Encourage girls to take risks during learning.
- Help girls recognize that mistakes happen, and that value can be derived from mistakes.
- Make sure that girls can participate in class without fear of put-downs.
- Encourage girls to be proud of their work. Don't allow them to apologize for their efforts as they present orally in class.
- Make learning meaningful with real-life applications for girls, strengthening their understanding of the world in which they live.
- Provide collaborative and cooperative learning opportunities to help girls share responsibility and develop trust.
- Provide competitive learning experiences—girls like to compete too!
- Provide opportunities to guide girls as they work individually, helping them see all they can do without others assisting them.
- Involve girls in higher-level thinking by employing good questioning techniques and giving recognition to girls when they ask good questions.
- Teach girls about alternative solutions—show that there is more than one way to approach a problem.
- Explain information, especially spatial and mechanical learning, with a variety of words and drawings to help all girls interpret and understand.

- Empower girls to realistically evaluate and judge the media messages they receive.
- Encourage girls to feel proud of their gender.

TEACHING WITH AN UNDERSTANDING OF GIRLS' INTERNAL LIVES

As we guide you through this chapter, we will help you address all the strategies for teaching girls in the box above. We will also guide you through an understanding of the inner lives of girls.

Girls benefit, just as boys do, from adequate space, good lighting, proper temperature, and a variety of seating options. Groups of girls often enjoy a cozier classroom environment than boys do, such as the one described earlier by Tameka Alexander, where they can bond with others, share experiences, and work collaboratively and cooperatively. They tend to learn better in quiet and more orderly classrooms. When girls are engaged in large group projects, they may require more classroom space as they design, build, and practice for presentations. They will also require room for movement activities and active learning, and many girls enjoy a sense of individual space for quiet study and reflection.

In their learning environments, girls need a variety of seating options and a variety of spaces designed for learning—cozy nooks for reading, creative spaces for writing, and centers for hands-on activities and investigation. They often need and enjoy spaces that are uncluttered and well organized for learning.

These are classroom basics, and as you guide your girls through their physical environment and their cognitive learning, you will note how much emotional life operates in a girls-only classroom. As one teacher put it, "Girls are complex in their emotions, and not the same as boys. Girls have very complex inner lives. You can say boys do too, and my two sons are certainly complex in their way, but if you've taught girls-only classrooms, you know what I mean—there is a lot going on in each of those young women." This teacher, like many others we've worked with, noticed that it is easier for boys to deal with peer issues and move beyond them, but girls harbor hurtful situations for longer periods of time, struggling to forgive and forget. This is just one example of their inner lives. Those inner lives have a great impact on their classroom.

During professional development sessions with teachers, we ask them to work in groups and come to consensus on "Things I Enjoy About Working with Girls" and "Things That Make Working with Girls a Challenge." The lists are invariably consistent—and these are the most common items on their lists:

Enjoy about girls...
- can read their writing
- more verbal
- turn in homework
- neater
- they can sit longer
- they try to please teacher
- they smell better!

Challenges about girls...
- cliques
- more drama
- hold grudges
- less assertive
- sneaky
- too talkative at times
- less willing to take risks

Do you notice something about these lists? The things we tend to enjoy about girls relate more to academic performance—things that may have an impact on grades and test scores, and things that tend to make a teacher's life easier!

How about the things that are a challenge? Though the items on this list tend not to have such a great impact on grades and test scores, especially in elementary levels, they do affect relationships and psychosocial development. They are also the things that can make girls' lives (and the lives of the adults around them!) more difficult as they move into middle and high school.

Understanding the Girl Code

Much has been written about "the boy code" and how boys frequently get subtle messages from an early age telling them that the only emotions they should reveal are their "masculine" emotions (anger, aggression, competition), never their sensitive sides. Many boys do all that they can to avoid appearing weak, showing their fear, or even their sorrow.

Girls are also limited by a "girl code." This code tells them that it is their responsibility to make others happy, to be "pleasers," willing to quickly give up something if they can improve a situation for someone else. If second grader Susan breaks her favorite red crayon, her classmate Julie may say, "You can have mine." If middle schooler Monique leaves her PE clothes at home for the third day in a row, her friend Cleo may lend hers to Monique, even though both girls are expected to dress for the same class. If seniors Margie and Jane are going out to lunch, it may be hard to decide where to go as both girls continue to say, "I don't care where we go, you choose."

Although actions like these may temporarily give a girl a better connection with peers, and they are laudable for their compassion and selflessness, they may also minimize a girl's long-term access to confident success. There is nothing wrong with being nice and trying to help others; however, what is the full message of "nice"? Too many girls believe it means being quiet, not showing anger or assertive behavior, and not expressing how they truly feel. Of course, while some are giving, others are taking, and often they do not switch roles. We don't want to see some girls so willing to please that they give up their confidence, while other girls wield so much power that they learn to treat others, including teachers, parents, and peers, with disrespect.

You may have noticed an illustration of the complex emotional lives of girls in their apologies. Many girls and women needlessly apologize. Sometimes it is for troubling someone whose job it is to assist them, as in "I'm sorry, but where do I find the science fiction section?" Then there are those girls who get up in front of the class to present a report or project and the first words they say are, "I'm sorry, but this is not very good." This is part of the girl code, and though it shows a well-behaved and giving child, it is interesting to note that once teachers in single-sex classrooms point out the negative effects of this code to female students, the girls often coach each other to a less "one-down" approach to tasks. In this example, for instance, a girl might call out, "Don't apologize—look how much time you spent preparing." The teacher might second that comment by asking the girls in the class, from that point on, not to apologize if they did in fact do the work.

This is just one subtle example of the opportunity we have in single-sex classrooms to focus upon teaching girls to express how they feel, and what they need, in ways that are fully and robustly respectful of their own and others' gifts. Through guided practice, teachers can help girls develop the necessary skills to be heard, while still being respectful and respected. In fostering the kind of classroom in which girls practice more assertiveness, teachers must also make no room for rudeness. Assertiveness does not mean forgiving negative behavior. When a girl makes a rude remark, the teacher can immediately ask her to repeat her message without attacking. As she does so, she can model a response for the girl that is not "overly nice" but not rude, either.

Drops in Female Self-Esteem

For the last twenty years, a number of studies have shown that many girls move through their later elementary school years and into puberty with lowered self-esteem and confidence. Whereas most students of both genders experience setbacks during these years of rapid growth and development, it seems that boys don't view their failures in the same way that girls do. When faced with disappointments, girls may begin to perceive themselves and their own "inadequacies" as the problem. This leads many girls into more negative, less optimistic attitudes, which further feeds the declining self-esteem and confidence cycle. Many girls will decide to stop participating in activities because they believe they will never be able to live up to the expectations they have for themselves. Their pessimism makes them less fun to be around, thus their popularity declines, as does their involvement with peers and activities, and the detrimental cycle continues.

In all classrooms, teachers can help girls through this cycle. In her fifth-grade class, teacher Mignon Mandon has noticed, "When things are upsetting socially for girls, they need opportunities to process verbally. They often tend to be more secretive than boys, especially with their social problems, and a problem can quickly escalate before adult awareness or intervention occurs." According to Mignon, "Girls need reassurance that it will be safe to talk things out and the understanding that by doing so they will likely be able to put things in perspective and move on." When she senses trouble for one or more girls, Mignon takes time in her class to hear from the girls about their emotional lives and their needs that day.

Like many teachers in girls' classrooms, Mignon has noticed that girls need:

- Words of encouragement to help them understand that things change, and that what seems so difficult this week may be much smaller next week.

- Optimistic strategies and problem solving that lighten the emotional loads. Taking time in the single-sex class for "teachable moments" serves girls in many positive and productive ways.

Understanding Girl Stress

Much of the emotional lives of girls relates to stress, and many of these stresses, which may go relatively unnoticed in a coed classroom, can be obvious in a class filled only with adolescent girls. We asked high school girls, "List things related to education and the future that stress you out." Some of their comments are instructive:

_____

"The combined effects of schoolwork, getting into college, and social issues make life stressful for teenagers."

—Kaitlin, 10th grade girl

"Difficult teachers and standardized tests are the worst."

—Marina, 12th grade girl

"I think it's hard to enjoy the present and still prepare successfully for the future. There are infinite decisions that we all know will affect the rest of our lives."

—Hannah, 10th grade girl

DID YOU KNOW? SEVEN KEY FACTORS CONTRIBUTE TO STRESS FOR GIRLS

Research indicates these key factors in adolescent female stress, with adolescence coming earlier and earlier for girls:

- Body image concerns
- Peer teasing
- Sexual harassment
- Relational aggression
- Bullying
- Drops in academic confidence
- Family problems, such as separation, divorce, mental illness, health issues, financial troubles

Girls develop a nascent sense of these stresses as early as age six; during puberty and adolescence one or more of them can become significant stressors. As you work in your single-sex classroom, especially if you are working in fifth grade and beyond, it can be instructive and essential to take the lists of stressors into the class and discuss each one with the girls. Often, the girls can divide into groups for a weeklong group project on how each of the items on the list stresses health and self-esteem. As the girls present their projects to the class, everyone becomes more closely bonded, and you as the teacher can wisely point out solutions the girls may not have considered.

Handling Relational Aggression and Girl Cliques in Single-Sex Classrooms

"Acts of relational aggression are common among girls in American schools. These acts can include rumor spreading, secret-divulging, alliance-building, backstabbing, ignoring, excluding from social groups and activities, verbally insulting, and using hostile body language (i.e., eye-rolling and smirking). Other behaviors include making fun of someone's clothes or appearance and bumping into someone on purpose. Many of these behaviors are quite common in girls' friendships, but when they occur repeatedly to one particular victim, they constitute bullying."

—National Association of School Psychologists

Lindsey, now in college, considers herself to be a good student. Her dream is to go on to medical school after college. She wrote us this story in an e-mail:

I was close friends with the other girls in my school's gifted program during elementary school, and I was really excited about going to middle school. But my friends seemed to change when we all got to sixth grade. Suddenly all they could talk about was boys and make-up and music videos. They sure didn't want to talk about homework! I tried to act interested because it seemed important to them, but it was so boring. Girls who had been my friends for years started avoiding me, making fun of my clothes and teasing me about being a "nerd" because I still studied a lot and really liked school. They stopped including me in their sleepovers and even avoided me in the lunchroom. They got a couple of boys in our same classes to call and pretend they liked me and ask me to sit with them at lunch, but then pretend they didn't know me and had never called. It was really embarrassing.

Lindsey was a victim of relational aggression by other girls. Luckily, she had a support system at home that she trusted and she made it through this painful time just fine, and is on track to realize her dream of becoming a doctor. She also took advantage of some optional girls-only classes where she found "discussion and relief from the part of the relational aggression that involved boys."

Relational aggression is a major cause of stress that tends to peak during the middle school years. Relational aggression is what "mean girls" do to other girls, attacking them in hurtful ways connected to their friendship circles. Often the instigator is motivated by jealousy, anger, a need for attention, or fear of competition. Girls may choose this type of bullying because it typically avoids being caught or held accountable. The most seemingly innocent girls may actually be the guiltiest. Girl bullies are often popular and perceived as favorites of adults. In your girls-only classroom, you are likely to have at least one girl who is a victim of relational aggression.

Because female self-esteem can be derailed by this kind of aggression, it is crucial to form one-on-one relationships with any girls you believe to be victims. It can also be crucial to question the girls about whether they are being cyberbullied. This kind of bullying is often not perceived by younger teen girls as being as dangerous as it can be.

Understanding Cyberbullying

Technology has provided a new platform for relational aggression, allowing girls (and boys) to use chat rooms (56 percent of cyberbullying), computer text messaging (49 percent), and e-mail (28 percent) to attack without having to face the victim. Why do they do it? In a 2005 research study by Dr. Sameer Hinduja at Florida Atlantic University and Dr. Justin W. Patchin at the University of Wisconsin-Eau Claire, 50 percent of cyber offenders say they "do it for fun." It wasn't fun for these girls:

Twelve-year-old girl from Massachusetts:

> *I have myself been bullied. It lowers my self-esteem. It makes me feel really crappy. It makes me walk around the rest of the day feeling worthless, like no one cares. It makes me very, very depressed.*

Sixteen-year-old girl from Alabama:

> *It's one thing when you get made fun of at school, but to be* **bullied** *in your own home via your computer is a disgusting thing for someone to do and I think anyone who gets kicks out of it is disgusting. It makes me feel badly about myself. It makes me wonder how people can be so rude and disrespectful of others and makes me lose faith in the human race. It decreases my self esteem and I often wonder what I did to make someone treat me that way.*

Fourteen-year-old girl from New Jersey:

> *Being bullied over the Internet is worse than anything. It's torment and hurts. They say "sticks and stones may break my bones, but words will never hurt me." That quote is a lie and I don't believe in it. Sticks and stones may cause nasty cuts and scars, but those cuts and scars will heal. Insultive words hurt and sometimes take forever to heal.*

Source: Hinduja & Patchin, 2009. Used with permission.

In their research, Hinduja and Patchin found that girls reported significantly greater negative responses to cyberbullying, with great feelings of "frustration, anger, and sadness." Unfortunately, 42 percent never talked to anyone about the bullying and 17 percent who were bullied admitted to bullying others. Dr. Hinduja and Dr. Patchin's complete research study can be accessed at www.cyberbullying.us/.

Helping Bullied Girls in Your Classroom

The single-sex classroom is a particularly opportune setting not only for helping girls who are the target of bullying by girls, but also helping girls harassed by boys. Girls' self-esteem is dramatically affected by remarks boys make to girls and about girls. For girls who may already lack self-confidence, situations like this will pull them down even further. In your classroom, you can make sure girls have sufficient information and talk time to understand and handle the situations that arise. When relationships and the emotional lives of girls start to interfere with school life, you can help girls understand their own brains, their self-development, their assets, and their need to come together as girls and women to care for one another. Specifically regarding boys, you can help girls understand that many of the behaviors they see in the other gender result from male puberty and male developmental culture, rather than from defectiveness in the girl herself. We live in a culture that focuses, to a great extent, on trying to get girls to think they are defective (we'll explore the media part of this problem in the next section). As girls learn in female teams that they are not defective, they make a significant passage into adulthood.

Healthy Living and Healthy Self-Images—Combating Messages from the Media

As you have no doubt noticed, far too many words and images in magazines and on TV are aimed at convincing girls that they should dress in provocative ways, that they should be thin, that they should focus a lot of energy and time on being sexy, and that these are the primary attributes that determine their worth. Teachers in the single-sex girls' classroom can certainly effect change as they provide opportunities for girls to examine the more legitimate sources from which their self-image and confidence should come. It can be very helpful to your girls if you can talk with them about makeup, clothing, and body image. A teacher in San Francisco gave us one formula that resonates for many teachers:

"Girls think their self-confidence comes from makeup, clothing, and material things. Part of my job is to help them see that self-confidence comes from accomplishments, caring, and self-respect."

> **TRY THIS: An Activity to Assess Media Messages**
>
> Find age-appropriate magazines and have students go through them, placing advertisements and articles in categories such as self-help, feature, fashion, makeup, hairstyles, boys, girls, self-knowledge, body image message, college, or career advice. Help students begin a process of determining what is negative, what is positive, what is manipulative, and which images are idealized and unrealistic.

In a culture obsessed with weight, beauty, and youth, where girls and boys receive so many unhealthy messages, teachers in girls-only classrooms can design curricula that help girls see a more realistic picture of body size, while teaching them the importance of healthy lifestyles, emphasizing good nutrition and exercise in the right proportions.

GIRL-FRIENDLY ACTIVITIES YOU CAN USE RIGHT NOW

Here are a number of activities and innovations developed by teachers of all-girl classrooms to help feed the desire for learning and challenge in girls.

- Start a girls' group, helping girls find ways to bond with other girls. This may be a hiking group, a creative writing group, a book club, a girls' science group, scout troop, a Girls on the Run® (www.girlsontherun.org) group, and so on. Anytime girls get together for a common purpose, they have an opportunity to understand and support each other.

- Help all girls understand "bullying mentality"—the role of the bully, the victim, and especially the role of the bystander(s)—by talking with them about each.

- Have your class read excerpts from books that address girls' issues and have discussions related to those issues, books such as: *Queen Bees and Wannabes* by Rosalind Wiseman; *Odd Girl Speaks Out* by Rachel Simmons.

- Plan instruction that shows girls the value of good nutrition and exercise and their effects on the brain and learning. Have girls create and perform original skits and songs that illustrate the important role that nutrients, good fats, essential vitamins and minerals, protein, amino acids, and glucose play in the proper functioning of the brain and the production of neurotransmitters. Highlight foods that are good sources to improve brain functioning.

- Get girls fascinated by science starting in the early grades with fun experiments that capture their imagination. Have a "girls-only" science fair for your single-sex girls' class; involve moms and bring in female scientists as motivational speakers.

- Find ways to provide sincere, constructive, and positive feedback to all girls, through teacher and peer comments.

- Encourage girls to act out scenes in books they are reading. They will be willing to share their emotions in dramatizations.

- Use trivia games and brain teasers to engage girls. Girls enjoy competition, too!

- Use journaling with girls, allowing them to connect what they read in novels to their own lives. This engages them in thinking about what is important and what they hope to represent as young women.

- Help girls discover their passions. Do your best to discover what each girl in your class loves to do. Plan activities that support their passions and allow girls to share their knowledge in those areas through projects which expand on their understanding.

- Celebrate! Find ways to recognize great moments for girls and acknowledge these through fun activities, skits, games, songs, and big hugs! Remember that some great moments happen when girls try something new or take a risk, not necessarily just when they win. Keep optimism a priority in your classroom!

INTEGRATING LEADERSHIP OPPORTUNITIES IN GIRL-FRIENDLY WAYS

"There has to be a recognition in society that there cannot be development and poverty eradication without a sustainable contribution of women.

The development of women is the biggest event for humanity yet to happen, for everybody."

————————————

—Phumzile Mlambo-Ngcuka, vice president of South Africa

From an early age, most girls learn to relate to others through empathetic encounters. Girls often try to lead by understanding the deep needs of others around them. This very natural spirit and energy in girls can be integrated into social leadership roles through social justice orientations in classrooms. It is never too early to get girls thinking about changing the world—starting a little at a time, and as future leaders of society. Girls-only classrooms can engage this approach without interference from adolescent boys who are trying to become leaders in their own way.

As you teach your girls-only classroom, look for opportunities to build leaders. Help girls have a sense that they are a part of a bigger world—that there is more going on than just what happens in school each day. Promoting social responsibility in girls will help them funnel their empathy in specific directions, convincing them that they can bring about change and influence others in positive ways.

TRY THIS: Develop Girls' Leadership Abilities

You can enhance girls' leadership abilities right now in a number of ways:

- Talk with girls about current leaders and how they handle their leadership responsibilities.

- Share examples of ways leaders have worked together to find cooperative solutions to problems.

- Meet with community leaders (the mayor, members of city council, leaders of special interest groups such as the Red Cross or United Way).

- Encourage and guide girls to take a greater leadership role in the classroom and in the school community.

- Ask girls what causes are important to them. You might be surprised that many girls have already been thinking and acting on their ideas, and it is powerful when girls share this with other girls.

- Help girls find community service projects, such as visiting the elderly, taking animal shelter pets for walks, cleaning up a park, or building a bench.

- Allow girls to make decisions and give them some control in choosing organizations to assist, such as Heifer International, the Salvation Army, food banks, and homeless shelters. If girls get to choose their participation, they are more likely to buy in and remain involved in enthusiastic ways.

- Research local issues, help girls interview community leaders on the various topics, and host a classroom candidate forum addressing the girls' concerns with prospective members of city or county government.

- Help girls learn about coalition groups that support women's and girls' issues. Teach girls about women in history who have led important causes, including causes supporting women's rights.

By the time girls reach preadolescence, they are often forming strong opinions about issues of social injustice. Girls who have learned in your classroom to stand up and speak out for what they believe will have broader perspectives and greater confidence, and will naturally put less emphasis on the day-to-day stresses of school and the sometimes insensitive behavior of their peers.

ENGAGING A GIRL'S COOPERATIVE SPIRIT

"When students participate in engaging learning activities in well-designed, supportive cooperative groups . . . , their brain scans show facilitated passage of information from the intake areas into the memory storage regions of the brain."

—Judy Willis, neurologist and teacher

As girls work together, you will discover that they are generally better than boys at interpreting emotions and reading facial expressions. They especially enjoy articulating their own emotions as they collaborate with other girls, reading the same book, listening to another girl's story or poem. They will readily discuss how they feel about a story, making such comments as, "When I was reading this part, I really started to feel sad and I wanted to call a friend to talk about how the story was affecting me."

Middle school teacher Sandy Pyeatt has learned how to set up her all-girl discussion groups for success. Through her experience of leading girls in Great Books-style discussions, Sandy is aware that girls struggle to know how to appropriately disagree with one another. They are frequently uncomfortable with being direct and at times feel overwhelmed with the need to be "nice." According to Sandy, "Girls often express their disagreements as if they are agreeing, when in reality, they aren't." Sandy encourages her students to be okay with disagreement and to respectfully share their thoughts and beliefs. To do this, she has established written guidelines to assist them.

TRY THIS: One Teacher's Principles for Respectfully Disagreeing

- Make sure the person knows you were really listening to what she said and trying to understand her point of view *before* voicing your disagreement. To do this:

  - Ask questions to better understand a particular thought or statement and the person's support for it.

  - Refer to things she said when you voice your thoughts.

- Disagree with the thought or statement, not with the person.

- Remember that you are working together to explore meaning. Respectful disagreement is probably the most effective way to do so, and thus, an important way to work together.

- Remember that it is not necessary to agree by the end of the discussion. You can agree to disagree and still have uncovered more meaning than if there had been no disagreement at all.

- Show that you are okay when others disagree with you by listening to them and trying to understand their point of view. Once you understand their point

---

> of view you can disagree "back," but do so by addressing the points they made with new thoughts and support, not just repeating and defending what you already said. Of course, you can also change your mind and agree with them or find some other meaning that builds on everything that has been said.
>
> • Remember that sometimes what feels like disagreement is actually an AND, not a BUT, situation.

Disagreement Starters That Aren't Disagreeable!

Sandy suggests the following:

• When _____ (a person) said _____, it made me think or wonder _____.

• I agree with _____ (part of a statement or thought); however, I disagree with _____ (another part of a statement or thought).

• I wonder if . . .

• What about . . . ?

• It's true that _____, however I also noticed _____ .

• I read, saw, or interpreted that differently from _____ (a person). I thought _____ .

Sandy's work with girls helps girls see that disagreeing is not a bad thing—that they can use their ears to hear another perspective, use their minds to consider all sides of an issue, and use their voice to share what they personally believe.

Some Tips for Noticing Group Dynamics Among Girls

In our work with girls-only classrooms, we've noticed that as they begin working in groups, some girls may not be particularly open to others' ideas. This kind of girl is likely to want the group to do things her way because she is convinced hers is the best way. Some girls like this manage to get their way through what may seem like kindness but is in fact manipulation of the group—they can be mean in a very polite voice. If repeatedly faced with this, many girls will decide to sit back and let others do the work, frustrated with always being assigned the less important group tasks and with never having their ideas accepted.

Teachers who are guiding group projects should try to notice this group dynamic right away. You can be present when girls initially work in groups, ready to help them see what they are doing. You can make sure the girls share the responsibilities fairly, assigning roles and tasks, and changing the roles that individual girls play as they move from project to project. It is important for every girl to make a valued contribution to group work and to be able to give you evaluative feedback on the process. When tensions build, you can step in to help girls cooperatively deal with the conflict.

Because we have found group self-assessment to be so helpful in girls' teams, we are providing you with assessment tools you can use in your cooperative group project. We hope you'll use these as you need them, and share any intriguing insights you gain.

Student Assessment of Cooperative Group Project

Strongly Agree	Agree	Undecided	Disagree	Strongly Disagree	Question
1	2	3	4	5	1. I enjoyed working with my cooperative learning partners.
1	2	3	4	5	2. I learned less working with this group than I would have learned independently.
1	2	3	4	5	3. Working with this group was difficult for me.
1	2	3	4	5	4. My group cooperated well to do this project.
1	2	3	4	5	5. I enjoyed my role in this group.
1	2	3	4	5	6. I did not contribute my fair share to this learning project.
1	2	3	4	5	7. My partners shared the responsibility for this assignment fairly.
1	2	3	4	5	8. My partners won't work out solutions with me when we need to figure something out or plan our next step.

Strongly Agree	Agree	Undecided	Disagree	Strongly Disagree	Question
1	2	3	4	5	9. I think my partners would rather work alone.
1	2	3	4	5	10. When we ran into problems as a group, my partners and I were able to find a solution.

All undecided (3 point) scores are added first (possible total of 30 points). Then to this score add the circled response numbers of the positively worded statements (statements 1, 4, 5, 7, and 10) and subtract from that score the circled response numbers of the negatively worded statements (statements 2, 3, 6, 8, and 9).

The lower the total score, the more positive the student felt about working with his or her group to complete the cooperative project. The higher the total score, the more negative the student felt about working with his or her group to complete the cooperative project.

Teacher Assessment of Student's Understanding of and Participation in Cooperative Group Project

Student Name: Cooperative Project:	Thorough Understanding Consistently and Actively	Good Understanding Without Prompting	Satisfactory Understanding With Occasional Prompting	Needs Improvement With Consistent Prompting
Works toward group goals				
Considers feelings and needs of all group members				
Accepts and fulfills his or her role as a group member				
Contributes personal knowledge, opinions, skills				

(Continued)

Teacher Assessment of Student's Understanding of and Participation in Cooperative Group Project *(Continued)*

Student Name: Cooperative Project:	Thorough Understanding Consistently and Actively	Good Understanding Without Prompting	Satisfactory Understanding With Occasional Prompting	Needs Improvement With Consistent Prompting
Values contribution of all group members and encourages everyone's participation				
Identifies needs and encourages action and change				

A Note About Competition

As you assess and utilize girls-only groups, you will probably see good moments for inserting competitive games, such as the kinds of competitive dynamics we described in the previous chapter on boy-friendly classrooms. Girls like to compete just as boys do, even though they may compete differently, and like to include somewhat less hierarchical competition into their learning experiences. Because the world is inherently competitive, it is crucial to choose some competitive frameworks within cooperative classrooms. Girls need more practice with competition than we may realize.

"Although we are seventh grade girls, and seventh grade girls have lots of girl problems, having just girls in our core classes has helped us get along. When we try to work out problems with friends and learn to compete, it helps not to have boys around

all the time. I can compete with the girls but also feel
closer to the girls and less self-conscious. We have
had opportunities to bond as girls and as friends."

—MacKenzie, 7th grade girl

Her simple language reveals a number of truths: that girls enjoy competing (this girl is a premier soccer player), that competing with girls and not boys provides a different sort of confidence and competitive experience, and that even when competing, girls are trying to bond in their own complex way. To an extent more subtle than with boys, cooperative learning among girls absorbs competitive learning into it, but often we must look very closely to find where competition begins and cooperation ends. With boys, the line is much more clearly drawn.

SUCCESSFUL TEACHERS OF GIRLS

"My favorite teacher is the perfect balance between
friend and authority figure. She can joke with us
and understand that we have responsibilities in
our lives besides her class. At the same time, she is
an excellent teacher and explains everything well,
earning respect from her students."

—Zoe, 12th grade girl

Teachers who value girls as individuals, and who listen to and support girls as a group, will truly enjoy the opportunities they have to encourage girls in and out of the classroom. If you expect the best from girls and encourage them to enjoy being smart, you can teach them that being smart means finding answers in whatever ways are needed, and in community with others.

Observations from Teachers of Girls

A middle school teacher told us about Sue:

> Sue is a very shy, extremely soft-spoken sixth-grade girl in my class. For the first month of school, I could not hear her, even when I was standing in front of her desk. I, and the class of girls, had to constantly encourage her to speak up. Today as she shared her group report, I suddenly realized that I could hear her. She was standing in front of the class and I was sitting in the back. It was clear that she has become more confident and relaxed in front of her all-girl peers.

Sue is a girl who needed extra encouragement from her class and from her teacher.

She was one of the girls you will meet who needs you as a teacher to give lots of affirmation. Sometimes male teachers, especially in the lower grades, provide less verbal encouragement than girls need to feel "brain-happy." Words mean a lot to girls (in both positive and negative ways). Successful teachers in girls-only classrooms often note the importance of verbal engagement.

Effective teachers of girls take girls' need for encouragement into consideration when asking questions. These teachers don't like to see a girl play the "helpless little girl" card. These teachers listen to and consider the purpose of the questions girls themselves ask. Are their questions seeking clarity? Are they helpful or simply a distraction? Less secure girls often ask questions simply to affirm they are doing the work correctly. In girls-only classrooms, a teacher has a chance to hone verbal skills infinitely without making the girl feel she is being "put down" in front of the boys. She (or he) can talk to girls about learning to ask good questions that will benefit their understanding and that of the group. They can model what makes a particular question a good one (genuinely expanding their own or everyone's understanding, helping see something in a different way). They can ask girls, as they are reading, to compose a good question for each chapter or each heading within a chapter, writing the question on a sticky note and placing it on the page where they got the idea for the question.

A teacher told us,

> I tell girls that I may not always answer their questions immediately. When a girl asks a question that I believe will get the class off task, I say, "I want you to think about that question (perhaps even write it down) and I will come back to you in a few minutes." I make sure that at some point I refer back to the questions I postponed—if I don't do this, the girls think I don't care about them and what they have to say.

Have a bulletin board area identified as the
"Parking Lot"
where students can post questions you agree
to "get back to later." This will help make sure
no one forgets!

Sometimes, I tell the girls to take the opportunity to find the answers on their own or in groups. I let the girls talk to a table mate or group partner to see if together they can answer the question. To be a successful teacher of girls, I've found that I sometimes have to help the girl see that she may already have the information to answer the question, if she will just look within.

This is a beautiful way of seeing and appreciating the subtleties of girls' minds, and working to help those minds advance into empowered leadership, and deep enjoyment of learning.

TRY THIS: Be an Effective Teacher of Girls

To be an effective teacher of girls, follow your instincts, and enjoy the spirit of girls. These tools may also be helpful in your tool box:

♀ Teach girls to ask good questions and analyze information carefully.

♀ Encourage girls to act independently.

♀ Discourage girls from needless apologizing.

♀ Teach girls to be mindful of their needs and not to ignore them.

♀ Give girls the opportunity to share their concerns and receive feedback.

♀ Teach girls to be assertive, yet respectful of the opinions and needs of others.

♀ Design curriculum and activities to help girls build on their language skills and enhance their spatial understanding.

♀ Seek to connect with girls in meaningful ways to enrich relationships.

♀ Use a variety of strategies to reconfigure groups of girls for activities, thus lessening girls' concern about clique relationships.

♀ Help girls locate the sources of their anger and channel it in more appropriate directions.

♀ Seek training to understand how gender issues affect girls and how to help girls understand and become authentic girls, not the media's interpretation of girls.

♀ Encourage girls to recognize their individual strengths and challenges.

♀ Handle girl issues as they arise, and use "teachable moments" to discuss the ethics of how to treat others.

♀ Challenge girls to gain self-respect and happiness by standing up on their own for what is right.

WRAPPING UP THE MAIN POINTS

Just as boy-friendly solutions can help girls, the girl-friendly solutions summarized here can help boys as well.

- Teach without gender bias
- Build self-esteem and confidence
- Help students be assertive in ways that are respectful
- Discourage pessimistic attitudes
- Use teachable moments for both instruction and emotional care
- Evaluate and respond to student stress
- Address bullying, including cyberbullying, and sexual harassment
- Teach media literacy and healthy lifestyles
- Address negative behavior in the classroom
- Help students ask good questions
- Use cooperative learning
- Encourage leadership in social justice

Strategies for Teaching Core Curricula to Boys

One looks back with appreciation to the brilliant teachers, but with gratitude to those who touched our human feelings. The curriculum is so much necessary raw material, but warmth is the vital element for the growing plant and for the soul of the child.

—Carl Jung

A mom from Vermont writes,

I have four sons, ages seven, eight, ten, and twelve, and I am constantly trying to figure "the school thing" out. They're all bright, according to their test scores, and yet school seems like a pointless exercise to them. I see all the little girls sitting nicely and learning—and I realize that no matter how bright my boys are they may never please the teachers the way girls do. Consequently, teachers like boys less—and they are given fewer opportunities in the classroom. Scholarships go to the students who excel in the system, the girls. I do hope that we as a culture begin to swing the pendulum back to the center and attend to the boys the way we have to the girls.

Moms, dads, and teachers of boys can relate to how this mother is feeling. Many bright boys are languishing in classrooms that just don't engage them, just don't seem to be able to take their boy energy and translate it into a love of learning!

In this chapter, we will specifically examine teaching boys the core subjects of math, science, language arts, and social studies, incorporating what we have learned about engaging the minds and bodies of boys in the classroom. From your years as a teacher and through your reading of the previous chapters in this book, we hope that you have been developing a vision of how to maximize male energy in any single-sex classroom—a vision that will set boys on an exciting course with a broad array of opportunities to help them succeed. Now we hope you'll bring that vision to bear specifically on core subjects.

TRY THIS: Tips for Raising Boys' Achievement in Core Classes

Teachers in boys-only classrooms have helped us develop this short list of ways to help boys learn core curricula:

- Deliver engaging lessons with a quick pace
- Break lessons into a number of bite-sized chunks
- Include a variety of active learning strategies—skits, role playing, investigations, hands-on activities, research, and the use of technology
- Include elements of challenge and plenty of competition
- As much as possible establish short-term goals and set time limits
- Allow social learning with a partner or a well-organized or structured group
- Include opportunities for listening, speaking, discussing, and guided writing

---

- Make sure assignments are relevant and meaningful to boys
- Give boys a real audience so that they can see the reason for employing their best effort and producing quality work
- Help boys transition between learning activities
- Include a time for review and reflection at the end of lessons
- Give positive feedback regularly

TEACHING CORE CURRICULA IN BOY-FRIENDLY WAYS

As you consider how to maximize core learning for boys, you can begin by looking at your students and wondering, "How can I help these boys become self-advocates for their own learning needs?" Boys want to meet challenges, and they want to buy into the way the challenge will be met. As early as you can, helping them become not just motivated but *self-motivated* can help boys know that they, too, shoulder the responsibility for making sure that learning situations work well for them.

Depending on the age of the boys in your core class, consider taking time to explain some of what we know about the characteristics of the male brain, telling boys that their classroom experiences will be planned to help them make the most of the way they learn. Once the boys understand why they are participating in single-sex instruction, they may begin to notice more about their own learning styles than they did before.

Consider asking the boys:

1. How do you learn best?
2. Was today's lesson easy for you to understand? Why? Why not?
3. What might have worked better?
4. Are you approaching this assignment in a way that works for you?
5. Are you taking care of your learning needs?

In Chapter Six of our book Strategies for Teaching Boys & Girls: Secondary Level *you will find a "Self-Assessment of Learning Style" that is a great tool to use with boys and girls. The tool was designed by Debra Engilman, Spanish teacher at Crespi Carmelite High School in Encino, California. It helps students understand their own and their classmates' learning styles so that they can work together more effectively.*

On a regular basis, spend time discussing which parts of the core lesson resonated with the boys, and which were less interesting and seemed less important. Be willing to make accommodations for boys. Allow them to stand up in the back of the room, sit on the floor, use stress balls, or even manipulate Play-Doh to help them focus; but remind them that accommodations only work if they do not disturb the learning of others.

Knowing that boys need to be more physically active and that their attention span tends to be shorter, you can plan class time accordingly, changing activities frequently, adding movement (see Chapter Five), and constantly evaluating whether a particular lesson or teaching method is effective. Less listening and more doing works far better for boys, especially in the crucial (and often tested) core curriculum areas. In general, when teaching core curricula to boys, teachers tend to replace some lectures with fast-moving lessons and activities.

TRY THIS: Provide Supervised Movement Time

Kim Carabo of Ewing Middle School allows her boys to stand and stretch just before they participate in a reading activity. They also do jumping jacks as well as leg and arm stretches. Kim sets one minute on a timer, and she participates in these movement activities with her boy students. When boys know there is a set time for the activity, "objectively" measured, they more readily accept that the activity is done.

As you teach core curricula, remember to set up your classroom to maximize the space for boys, allowing them room to work together and separately. Boys can come to really enjoy the single-sex environment, and that enjoyment can itself affect their learning. They can learn to appreciate appropriate class procedures and expectations, and value the teacher who seeks to understand them and works to meet their learning needs.

Think about changing "Class Rules" to "Classroom Procedures." Boys will be inclined to break rules, but they will be inclined to follow procedures!

> **TRY THIS: An "On Time and Ready to Learn" Innovation**
>
> Sandy Pyeatt uses a little "friendly competition" with her sixth-grade boys to encourage them to get to class on time with all the materials they need. Each day she greets boys upon their arrival to class, and quickly awards a star to each one who gets there on time with all his books and supplies. The boys place their stars on a poster, and as soon as every boy in the class has received twenty stars, they get a small celebration (usually a game outside for the last ten minutes of class). Then the process begins again. Stars create competition, but Sandy notices that the boys encourage each other in friendly ways to get to class and be ready to start on time. According to Sandy, "It is lighthearted competition that works!"

Providing competition, space, expectations, movement—these are just a few of the things you can do to help boys engage in learning itself, and thus in your core curricula. These are the foundation of a boy-friendly learning environment. Let's look closely at a number of other key innovations and areas of focus. Each of these has been explored and utilized by teachers of core curricula in single-sex classes.

Giving Instruction and Directions to Boys

Teachers often report that boys in their classes do not want to appear "stupid" in front of peers or teachers. Boys who perceive themselves as frequently being "the stupid one," will lose much of their motivation to learn. To help them avoid this, it is crucial that you give them very clear instructions, never assuming that they understand things in the same way as girls. Boys do not often "read between the lines" the way girls do—contemplating unspoken expectations can trip boys up, causing them to feel foolish and embarrassed. Though all teachers need to be aware of this, female teachers are more likely to make such mistakes with boys. We should remember that boys tend not to hear as well as girls and that they learn best using their strongest sense—vision. Boys benefit most from seeing information, so use the board and overhead projector.

The more that teachers can visually share examples of good work in advance with boys, the more likely boys will be to achieve the expected standard in terms of the quantity of their words and the quality of their presentation.

Joe Kirstein, a science and math teacher working with boys, tries to limit verbal instruction in his seventh-grade boys' classes to ten minutes or less. He uses lots of visual cues, and chooses to allow more time for students to learn through investigation and exploration. Joe follows his brief presentations with activities—individual and group—that allow boys to move within the classroom. To make sure that students understand their assignments, he chooses a different boy each day to repeat and explain the directions and procedures to the group in "boy" words. That boy may also ask another boy to help when he is confused.

Boys function best in a classroom when they know in advance what is happening. When there is a visible plan, boys don't have to wonder what is coming next. They will be ready to focus on their work and less likely to complain as they transition to the next topic. Teachers often hear boys make such statements as, "Do we have to do this? or "Can't we do something else?"—but when boys know there is a plan, they are less likely to question what they are asked to do.

Ultimately, giving boys a visual schedule with specific time references will help them meet the goals you have for them during a designated period of time; carefully watching their follow-through will tend to avoid later issues.

Here is an example of what a teacher might display on the board for a forty-five-minute geography or science class:

Using numbers—clocks or other quantifiers—for boys' tasks helps them work within a specific time frame and serves as practice as they learn to budget their time for individual assignments, both in and out of class. Some boys need extra

> **Good morning--let's get started!**
>
> 9:00 - Record homework in planner
>   Work with your map project group,
>   put final touches on government
>   mind map
>   Make sure each person knows his
>   responsibility
> 9:10 - Final practice with your group - keep the
>   presentation in your 2-minute time limit
> 9:25 - A quick Brain Gym activity - leaders for
>   today are Joey and Mark
> 9:30 - Presentations!

assistance in developing their time-management skills, learning to approach their assignments in realistic ways that keep them from being overwhelmed by work. These skills will reduce procrastination and ideally make homework a less daunting task.

Helping Boys Transition Between Learning Tasks

Moving effectively from one activity to another is more challenging for boys than for girls. How often do boys jump up to do something before the teacher finishes giving all the directions? Though they may quickly get to their feet at the mere suggestion of a change in activity, they can also forget to listen to the remaining instructions, lose their focus, and get involved in unproductive chatter or playful activities. Boys struggle to stop what they are doing, clean up, put things away, and get ready for what comes next. Teachers can help by developing strategies that make these transitions easier for their male students.

Some teachers in language arts have used music and movement as transitional elements, with great success. Following morning snack time in her fifth-grade classroom, Mignon Mandon plays quiet classical music and has her students do stretches for movement and to help them refocus. Mignon says, "I started the year leading the stretches to music, and then when students became comfortable with them, they volunteered to lead them too. It really helps the boys quiet their bodies and get ready to work. The music keeps them quite focused."

Third-grade teacher Rachael Ide uses the following activity to provide movement and musical refocusing of her writing students. She calls it the **Hot Color Game**. Rachael plays the song "Hot, Hot, Hot" while the students dance and move around the room to find an object of a specific color. Rachael says,

> When I tell students we are going to play the Hot Color Game, they immediately stand up, and I instruct them to find an object that is "blue" (or yellow, or green, and so on). Then I turn the music on for a few seconds, and when I stop the song, each child is standing somewhere in the room, touching the object that is blue. I repeat this a few times, each time changing the color. When I am ready to end the game, I ask them to find an object that has their name on it (like their desks), and they sit down when the music goes off, ready to get back to work.

Rachael takes the use of music even further than its role as an accompaniment to movement. She tells her students, "When you hear the music, turn to page ninety-eight in your book" or "When the music plays, take out the story you began writing yesterday." Knowing that music can actually change mental states, she chooses songs for specific purposes and lets students enjoy them for a minute or so, and while they are listening, they are also getting ready, taking out their book, or turning to the appropriate page. Often they are also singing along or even dancing beside their desks, but when she turns off the music they are ready to go.

HELPING BOYS IN MATH CLASS

Boys are often predisposed to spatial tasks, so they often enjoy working with symbols, diagrams, maps, and abstractions. When math is taught on the blackboard rather than in a wordy textbook, boys tend to engage to a much greater degree—because they are visual and their spatial brains get it!

Although boys often "get math," they are frequently not as willing as girls to effectively apply what they know about math. Boys can be impatient, seeking to understand a concept quickly, but then reluctant to practice the concept for mastery. Many do not like writing out the steps needed to solve a problem—preferring to do the work in their heads and sometimes making numerous careless errors in the process.

One seventh-grade pre-algebra teacher illustrated this: he told us his boys-only class gets bored when he tries to demonstrate too many example problems as he introduces a new concept. He reported, "They just want to learn the basics. Then they are ready to begin trying to solve the problems on their own."

Although the boys do make more careless errors and submit less accurate work than his girls' class, he says, "Boys seem to have a greater understanding of the process they are following and they can more easily apply it when they encounter similar situations that arise days later." This asset can become a focus for teaching boys how to apply math to their real world. We want boys to understand the value of what they learn in math and how it might help them in the future, but they frequently have little patience for trying to get all the steps correct in the process. Teachers can help boys see the future value of a math problem by relating the problem to a boys' interests. For instance, there is a lot of math involved in getting your home connected to the Internet (cost per month, deposits to pay, what rate of speed do you want your connection to be), and you need the Internet if you want to visit MySpace!

Helping Boys Develop Confidence in Math

Karla Weidner, sixth-grade math and science teacher, notices that her boys and girls are different in terms of how they express their confidence in math. She tells us:

> One of my boys completed an assignment that wasn't due until the following day, but asked if he could hand it in early. As he gave me his work, I noticed that he had missed two of the first three questions. When I explained to him that he had missed some of the first few questions and suggested that he take the assignment home to check his work, he said, "Well, I'm pretty sure I got the rest of them right!" I don't think he was being lazy. He really did think he had done all of the problems correctly. I often see that the boys I teach are over-confident in their math ability, and hence prepare less for tests, while the girls are less confident and will spend more time preparing and

studying for math tests. I think this is why the girls' test averages are typically higher than the boys.

To help boys do more of their assignments and do better with follow-through, Karla uses this innovation:

> In my classes I have students use small white boards to solve problems at their desks and show me their work. This is how I get a quick assessment of their understanding. Occasionally I have given a problem, had the students work it on their white boards, and then said, "If you are really confident in your answer stand up. If not, stay seated." I stopped doing this because almost ALL of the boys will stand up and none of the girls will, even though there is no significant difference in the number of correct answers between the boys' classes and girls' classes.

Using Competition in the Boys' Math Class

Math teacher Joe Kirstein told us, "Boys seem to crave competition, so we sometimes play **Krypto**, a competitive math card game." In the game, the players select five Krypto cards (their hand) and they must use each card once. They also select a sixth card (the answer). They are expected to apply the four basic arithmetic operations to these numbers until they get the answer (from the sixth card). The boys get points based on the number of operations they use.

Brian Bilek is a geometry teacher at Crespi Carmelite High School. He employs competition in his class, setting up carefully selected table groups with specific objectives that also help with classroom management. These are the early phases of a game he uses with the boys called **Basketball Math**.

At the beginning of each chapter, Brian uses the most recent test grades of his

geometry students, along with a few other factors, to assign boys to table groups that are academically balanced with the other table groups. He also takes into consideration each student's behavior, in an effort to position students in groups that will minimize classroom distractions. Because Brian encourages group work and cooperative learning, it is important that the members of each table be able to work well together.

During the unit of study, the table groups acquire positive and negative points on a scoreboard displayed in the front of the classroom. Teams can receive positive points for good behavior and negative points for being off task. The teams also get points based on how many "bathroom breaks" they have not used. Each table receives four opportunities for student bathroom breaks at the start of each new chapter. When a student needs to use the restroom, his table uses up one of their bathroom breaks. If they need more than four bathroom breaks, the table starts to acquire negative points.

Most points are earned through "table challenges." Brian gives each table group problems to work on, and the table that finishes the problems correctly first receives three points; second, two points; and third, one point. The rules for each challenge can change, but the example mentioned is fairly standard. The tables also receive points for keeping their area and table clean.

On the day of the chapter review, the class plays the game of Basketball Math. Each team starts with their overall score, determined by subtracting negative points from positive points accumulated during the chapter unit. Then each student receives a review worksheet to complete with his group. After the groups have had a chance to complete their worksheets, the game begins. Starting at table one, Brian asks for the answer to a particular question. If the group gets the answer wrong, then it is the next table's turn. If the second table group gets it right, then each boy at that table has the chance to shoot a basketball for one point, two points, or three points based on the distance of the shot. These points are added to the group's overall table score. At the end of the game, each member of the team with the most points receives five extra credit points for the chapter test; second place gets four points, and so forth.

Using Football to Teach Math

Dr. Gary Ross, who was a long-time math teacher before becoming a principal, shares two of his favorite boy-friendly math activities:

"In the south, football is big and the boys really enjoy discussing and playing football. To engage them with math, I often find ways to relate football to the math concept being studied. For example, in helping my boys see and better understand the process of adding negative and positive integers, I use the football field to teach them. If on second down a team begins at the twenty-five yard line on their side of the field, gains five yards and also gets a fifteen-yard penalty, where would they begin their progress for third down?"

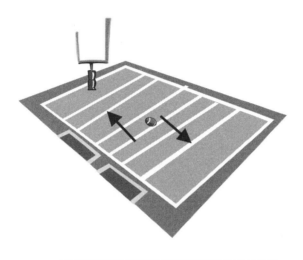

If on second down a team begins at the twenty-five yard line on their side of the field, gains five yards and also gets a fifteen-yard penalty, where would they begin their progress for third down?

Dr. Ross finds that boys are good at graphing coordinate points, but to add practice and improve their understanding, he sets up a Battleship-type game in the classroom, in which the boys have to let him know if the coordinates he gives them actually lead to the Battleship.

Using Physical Games to Help with Math Learning

Math teacher Charlotte Greene frequently sends her boys to the board to solve problems. According to Charlotte, they really like to be out of their seats doing

math together, and she adds an element of fun and competition by giving the boys a chance to shoot a soft ball into a small empty trash can for each math problem they get correct on the board. If they get two problems out of three correct, they get two shots at putting the ball in the trash can. The boys love this and it helps them focus on doing problems carefully and correctly.

"My students love to move around in math class and they remember more when they do these activities."

—Crystal Fowler, Ewing Middle School

HELPING BOYS LEARN SCIENCE

Boys in general love to do, build, and explore—all elements of science learning. When given the opportunity to do hands-on, interactive work in science, boys are likely to be fully engaged in their learning. Boys build their science skills and knowledge not as much from reading or hearing about science as they do from experiencing it. They find meaning in relating their science lessons to the world around them. Boys are naturally curious about their world and need a wide variety of science activities throughout their school years that keep them excited and encourage their curiosity.

"The grandmother of one of my students became a 'Lab Mom.' She came to my classes during labs. She helped with the boys, showing them how to fold their aprons and clean up their areas (lab stations). She also helped me set up labs.

The greatest experience was the lab on mixtures. We made butter. The grandmother came as usual on that lab day. There were two classes of ninth-grade boys and after the labs she took a pound of butter from each lab and made a pound cake for each class. The boys were very good and had a great deal of fun. She tied [making the cakes] to the prior lesson on measurement.

She talked about the measurement of the different substances that she put in the cakes. Last she demonstrated how to cut the cake to get twenty-four pieces. Delicious!"

—Frances Hendrix, Hope High School

Project-Based Learning and Science

More and more schools are using project-based learning in their programs and discovering the tremendous difference it can make to boys' motivational levels. Project-based learning changes the traditional teacher-centered classroom into a classroom where student interest becomes the focus. This innovative approach allows the standard curriculum to become engaging and interdisciplinary. During the project-based lessons, the teacher becomes a coach and a facilitator, learning alongside students and developing stronger relationships with them. Students work together to pursue their interests, while developing collaborative skills, designing their own projects, incorporating various technologies, and learning in-depth information on a particular topic.

By its very nature, project-based learning also requires an alternative means of assessment—not a written test, but a display of a result. This is great for boys. The projects and evaluations can be limitless in their scope, and teachers can find many opportunities to partner with other schools for research, even on a global level.

"If I wanted to become a better carpenter, I'd go find a good carpenter, and . . . work with this carpenter. . . . And that's how I'll get to be a better carpenter. So if I want to be a better learner, I'll go find somebody who's a good learner and with this person do some learning. But this is the opposite of what we do in our schools. We don't allow the teacher to do any learning. We don't allow the kids to have the experience of learning with the teacher because that's incompatible with the concept of the curriculum where what is being taught is what's already known."

—Seymour Papert, interview on Project-Based Learning
(www.edutopia.org)

TRY THIS: Ideas You Can Use for Project-Based Science

Try one or more of these ideas in your boys-only science class. The results may startle you—and highly engage the boys. Have your students

- Research local science topics that are of interest in your community, such as factory pollution, the effects of construction, or wildlife concerns. Conduct interviews with local agencies, experts, and politicians. Take digital photos that support the concern, write articles to the newspaper, and debate the topics.

- After studying water quality and speaking to experts on the topic, choose two lakes or two streams near your school, secure water samples from both, and assess the water quality. Gather data. Identify and compare the organisms present in the water. Draw inferences. Question findings. Post the results.

- Develop a project on environmental degradation. Use graphics. Write stories, essays, or letters. Have a discussion forum.

- Partner with students in another country to investigate a science issue common to both areas. Create a Web site to share information and photographs.

- Have each student choose an endangered species to research and then prepare a presentation illustrating the plight of that species. In small groups, write skits, poems, or songs that can be presented to parents at an Endangered Species Fair.

- Become weather experts, doing daily reports on local weather for your school. Report on temperature, precipitation, barometric pressure, and cloud types. Learn about weather phenomena that may affect your area or other global areas (monsoons, blizzards, tornados, hurricanes).

- Investigate solar energy. Visit a home or business that uses solar energy as its primary energy source. Build miniature solar homes using cardboard, plastic, aluminum foil, rocks, or other materials. Have a competition to see which structure will produce the highest temperature when placed outside on a sunny day.

- Learn about the brain. Help boys gain a better understanding of how their brains function and how their brains are wired differently from girls' brains.

> Research the latest information on the human brain and design projects to share understanding of the function of the lobes of the brain, how memory is stored, how messages are received, and the roles of neurons and neurotransmitters. Investigate how diet, exercise, and stress affect the functioning of the brain. Use charts, models, PowerPoint presentations, and skits to share the information. (A great resource for helping students learn about their brain is Dr. Daniel Amen's curriculum, Making a Good Brain Great! Check the Sources section to find more information on this curriculum.)

HELPING BOYS GAIN LITERACY SKILLS

Eighth-grade language arts teacher Kim Carabo says, "When I taught in a mixed-gender classroom, I could not get my boys to actively participate in class discussions. They didn't want to read in literature or even look like they liked to read. Now that there are no girls, boys are more competitive with grades and answering questions out loud. They like to be in charge and be important in their group. They are reading and writing more."

When it comes to reading and writing, some boys perceive these topics as feminine and go to great lengths to avoid them. They find them boring and believe that if they do show interest in these subjects, their friends might make fun of them. They believe they are not good at reading and writing, and because they think they cannot win, they have little desire to compete in these areas with girls. For many reasons, boys see these subjects as obstacles to their success.

Boys and Literacy—Building a Culture of Reading for Boys

"I don't really read that much—I wish I did though. I don't read at school. At home, I read philosophy, reviews of movies/music, history-related texts, and Gary Larson calendars."

—Wayne, 12th grade boy

There are boys who love to read, boys who are willing to read, and boys who seek out books. Still, many boys are reluctant to read, and research on gender and literacy tells us:

- Boys often value reading less than girls do.
- Boys often lag behind girls, taking longer to learn to read and reading much less than girls do.
- Boys tend to understand less of what they read, especially when reading fiction.
- During boys' early years in school, few of them think of themselves as "non-readers," but by high school well over half of them do.
- When boys perceive a book as "too feminine," they avoid it.

Though literacy statistics can seem daunting, your language arts class can meet its challenges using boy-friendly strategies.

One crucial step you can take is to broaden your school's understanding of literacy. Many boys who don't like novels are quite literate in their use of other sources (information books, magazines, and Internet sites). Boys are seldom assisted in connecting this other reading with literacy, and you can help them develop a clearer sense of what literacy is to them.

At the same time, you have to get them to read books. A primary way of doing that is awareness of what boys like to read in books. Some of the elements that boys look for in books are:

- Characters that help them visualize and make connections to the past
- Fearless, brave, and heroic characters who can survive thrilling, daring, and incredible circumstances
- Monsters and things that give them "the willies"
- Heroes who battle evil
- Mysteries, cliff-hangers, suspense and intrigue, thrillers, detective stories—more action than emotion
- Stories and characters they can identify with in terms of what they themselves like to do or hope to become

- Fantasy and science fiction—including time travel, space travel, life on distant planets, destroying aliens with laser weapons
- Characters with a sense of mischief, taboo subjects, and madcap mayhem
- Slapstick, humorous, off-the-wall silly things, including pranks and mayhem
- Characters who break out of the restrictions that boys feel in terms of expectations for behavior
- Places they have never imagined and things that dazzle their minds and expand their world
- Books that include strange facts and information—great topics to discuss with friends!
- Comics and illustrations (graphic novels)
- Stories about war and military combat; armed forces, weapons, military jets, submarines
- Stories that bring history to life: medieval times of knights and castles; ancient times of dinosaurs; adventures in history such as our country's westward expansion
- Stories that depict the trials and tribulations of athletes (sports biographies), helping boys gain knowledge about statistics and sports terminology. (Surprisingly, sports novels do not deliver for all boys—for some, reading the book may not equate to playing the game.)

"When we are encouraging boys to invest their time and effort in something they have so far seemed reluctant to do, we should consult them sincerely about what they might actually want to read. Then there is a chance they will see that, hey, reading is all right, reading is cool fun, reading can be full of the stuff that appeals to them, makes them laugh, makes them recoil with the cry, 'That's gross,' and makes them quickly thrust the book under the nose of a mate with the words, 'Hey, you gotta read this.'"

—James Moloney

If you can help boys find books that fit the list of what they already read, the literacy of boys in your class will increase.

Meanwhile, there may also be certain district-required or school-required books of more depth and literary significance that your boys must read. These books often explore the lives of characters through their emotional experiences and expose boys to positive male (as well as female) role models. These books are honest, moral, responsible, and courageous, and boys need their messages.

For boys ages nine to twelve, these books are often better received when read to them. Boys of this age can more easily accept, be interested in, learn from, and value this type of material when the experience is shared with an adult. When an adult reads a thoughtfully selected book to a boy, explaining subtleties along the way, he or she can help build a culture of reading, encouraging a boy's interest and perhaps even his passion for books. Boys who have frequent opportunities to share reading experiences with an adult will eventually replace being read to with the opportunity to read on their own.

For the later age groups, reading aloud is still fine, but now the high school class reads the book aloud, in turns. If the boys can also act out the book, even better. Many language arts teachers in middle and high school are having boys create dramas about the hard-to-read books. This engages boys' spirits in what they read.

And as always, it can't hurt to be aware of resources that already list books boys like. Here are some:

- *Books for Boys* by Michael Sullivan, author of *Connecting Boys With Books* (www.geocities.com/talestoldtall/BooksforBoys.html)
- *Great Books for Boys* by Kathleen Odean
- *What Stories Does My Son Need?* by Michael Gurian and Terry Trueman
- James Moloney's "List of Sure-Fire Winners—Books not to be read to boys—because they will happily read them on their own" (www.home.gil.com.au/~cbcqld/moloney/books7.htm)
- Guys Read by Jon Scieszka (www.guysread.com)

TRY THIS: Ways to Promote Reading Among Boys

Here are some highly successful strategies you can use right now.

- Build a boy-friendly collection of books in your classroom, including non-fiction, how-to books, magazines, newspapers, comic books, joke books, books about hobbies and sports.

- Invite fathers or male community members into the classroom to have book talks about their favorite book(s) or to read to boys. This helps dispel boys' notion that it is not manly to read.

- Work with the librarian to plan special programs in the library for boys (such as a martial arts presentation) and make sure that books on the topic are on display for boys to check out and read.

- Ask the librarian to put boy-friendly posters on the walls and boy-friendly books near the library computers, where boys hang out.

- Encourage boys and men to become library volunteers. Get coaches and athletes involved in read-alouds for boys.

- Read fiction and nonfiction books aloud.

- Have boys respond to what they read through art.

- Provide boys with a buddy reading program—older boys with younger boys, or peers who read the same book and have book discussions.

- Read the newspaper with boys.

- At Halloween, package favorite mystery books in black bags the students have decorated. Attach a spooky written review of each book on the outside of the bag. Let students choose books to take home and read.

- Have boys read about their favorite sports team and write a review of how the team is doing this year.

- Engage boys in inquiry-based instruction for reading purposes. Use teacher- or student-generated questions on a particular topic to get boys interested in exploring or investigating a topic in depth. For example, have boys read a short article on "black holes," and then formulate their own questions about this topic for further inquiry and research.

- Create a "boys-only" zone in the library where boys can talk about books they have enjoyed and see books other boys have enjoyed too.

- Use drama as a means of getting boys to engage emotionally with what they read. Don't assume that boys won't dress up to do skits, especially now that girls are not in the classroom. Give boys a box of fabric, some large pieces of felt, and a stapler to fasten things together, and you'll be amazed at what they will create!

- Set manageable reading goals for classes and find ways to celebrate when readers meet their goals.

- Have a male teacher sponsor a book club for boys.

SUCCESS STORIES FROM LANGUAGE ARTS TEACHERS

Dave Curtis, a teacher in a single-sex boys' fifth-grade class, has some unique ways of engaging his students in doing book reports. "Instead of the usual book report the boys create a cereal box based on the book. Sometimes I give them clay and they 'show me' something about the book. Today I wanted to know if they were getting the Bill of Rights we'd been reading about, so I gave them a piece of paper and asked them to create a comic strip showing understanding of an Amendment. The ability to turn information into their own words was proof they got the material."

When she first started teaching a single-sex boys' kindergarten class, Tessa Michaelos struggled to find ways to get her boys just to pick up a book to read, much less take one home. She began to change her classroom library to include books that would interest boys, adding books about karate, basketball, and other topics toward which boys seemed to gravitate. She made a big deal about books, building them up in a dramatic way. Tess had the idea of having her boys make their own books, and it wasn't long before she noticed that whenever a visitor entered the room, the boys would quickly direct the visitor to the classroom library and share the books they had made.

Kim Carabo of Ewing Middle School uses books that her more reluctant eighth-grade readers can relate to. Her students love the **Bluford series**, which takes place in a predominantly African American urban high school. The Bluford stories are about students who cope with problems that many students face, such

as gangs, absenteeism, and challenging family relationships. It is a very popular series whose fictional characters are easy for students to relate to in very real ways.

Carolyn Bittinger teaches two classes of Ramp Up to Advanced Literacy (a program that was designed to accelerate the academic achievement of middle and high school students) for freshman boys at Hope High School. Carolyn shared this story:

> This is the first year that I have taught gender specific classes, and I have to say that I have really enjoyed it. The boys from my Ramp Up classes participated in cross-age tutoring last month at Clinton Primary School. My male students diligently prepared for this event before reading to the first-graders, and all of them did a fantastic job. Because my classes include only male students, I feel that it was easier for them to practice reading children's picture books out loud to each other. There was certainly a lot of laughter, and there were embarrassing moments for my guys in preparation, but they overcame these obstacles. They even expressed to me that it was easier because the girls were not around when they made the funny character voices and sounds. I am extremely proud of my guys.

HELPING BOYS BECOME BETTER WRITERS

"One time that I really liked writing was when I got to write a free story and it didn't get edited. Sometimes when it's edited it can get frustrating. Sometimes when people edit it, they tell you what to write about and, no, this is wrong."

—Samuel, 4th grader

Writing is the area of study that seems to create the most problems for boys, and the single-sex classroom can enable teachers to specifically target this concern. As with reading, boys are performing significantly lower than girls on tests that measure writing, and the gap is disturbing. Though teachers would agree that boys in their classes (with some exceptions) are generally weaker in writing than girls, they are also noticing messages boys are receiving that turn them off to writing. These messages are from a variety of sources—the media, stereotypes from pop culture, responses from teachers to written assignments—and can promote disdain for writing as well as reading. It is possible, even probable, that predetermined judgments about boys' writing significantly diminish their interest in producing written language. Helping boys become better writers requires vigilance and innovation.

Using Technology

Billy Rook is a teacher and coach at Hope High School, and uses technology to get his freshman boys excited about writing. He tells us:

> In my ninth-grade civics class I have all boys. I have been able to get them to write essays using two techniques I obtained during an initial training session. The techniques deal with technology and competition. My laptop has the Windows Journal Tablet—boys can come up

and write on the tablet and project it on the screen for the class to see. We have been writing class essays.

To begin this activity, one boy writes a sentence and a different person adds the next sentence, constructing the essay. It becomes very competitive to be the next person to write! They must first tell me the sentence they would add next before they can write it on the tablet. They have created wonderful essays as a class. I "weaned" them from one sentence each to one paragraph each. Next, they will be writing full essays on their own. I am excited about the quality of the work being produced compared to the level produced at the beginning of the semester. The boys now ask as they come into class, "Are we going to write today?"

With their less-developed fine motor skills, many boys struggle with the physical act of writing from early on. Fortunately, technology now offers some assistance in this area, and parents and teachers can make sure that students who struggle with handwriting are provided the necessary computer hardware, software, and training to more successfully put their words on paper.

Using High-Interest Topics

When asked to write, a few boys will love it, some will endure it, and others will shut down, refusing to give writing a chance. Many teachers struggle to get what they consider quality writing from boys. Often the prompts that are given to students to get them writing are more "girl friendly" than "boy friendly." To improve this, teachers can encourage high-interest writing topics for boys. If a boy is not engaged in the topic he is exploring, you can help him adjust the topic or change it. We must realize that it is often a waste of our own and our boys' time to expect them to do a good job writing about a topic that does not interest them in the least. The more we let boys choose their topics, the better writing we will get from them, even if that means they don't write about a novel, but instead write about computer games and instant messaging.

Teaching Foundational Skills First

Although many of the challenges boys face as writers are directly related to their attitudes regarding writing, many boys come into your classroom lacking basic and fundamental writing skills. These skills include:

- Generating ideas for writing
- Using their words to put ideas into meaningful sentences
- Developing their thoughts into paragraphs with strong topic sentences
- Organizing their paragraphs into meaningful papers
- Revising and editing their work, using correct spelling, grammar, and punctuation

For the first month of class, you may want to provide opportunities for good writers to tutor students for whom writing is more of a challenge—always remembering that some students (and their parents) are not interested in tutoring, so be careful to make this a voluntary activity with no pressure to participate. Encourage outside mentors, especially males, to come in and work with struggling students whenever possible.

TRY THIS: Strategies to Promote Writing Among Boys

These strategies are quite widely used in boys-only classrooms. You may be able to put some to use right away. Some teach the basics, and some take writing further.

- Help boys find fun ideas that engage their imagination. Share your own interesting, fun stories to help boys develop theirs.

- Involve a social component with each writing assignment, such as sharing writing with the class or with a peer—if you do this, boys often enjoy the process more.

- Model good writing for boys to give them images and lead them in the direction you want them to go. Explanations about the importance of including detail may not work as well as simply giving the example of "The red car drove around the corner at sixty miles an hour." If you model the detailed sentence, the boy can often more easily write with detail.

- Use teacher-created templates to explain writing requirements to boys (number of pages required, headings required, number of sentences needed to make a good paragraph, and so on.) Boys need specific guidelines to follow.

- Allow boys to write their first draft without worrying about mechanics. Try not to respond negatively to their original drafts. Look for the good and highlight that, finding ways to subtly assist boys toward a higher level of achievement. Ask questions to engage the writer in a thought process that makes him feel that the "new thinking" that comes from a writing conference with the teacher is really his own.

- Allow boys to polish their best pieces, but do not require that they do this with everything they write. Though they need to work on spelling, organization, neatness, and so forth, they will do this better and more readily on a piece that they feel is worthy of this level of revision.

- When grading writing, give separate grades for the way boys express their ideas and the way they employ appropriate writing mechanics. By separating the two grades, the teacher should be able to convey to the boy that his ideas are valued, thus encouraging his motivation to write, while also indicating that he still needs to improve the mechanics.

Many boys, by nature, use fewer words than girls. Try these strategies often to improve word production and word use:

- Provide opportunities for boys to discuss ideas before they begin putting words to paper.

- Have boys brainstorm writing ideas on a specific topic in small table groups (2–3 boys) with each boy recording single ideas for writing on two-inch sticky notes (one idea per sticky note). The boys should place these notes in the center of the table then organize their many ideas into related groups. With several minds working together, sharing ideas on a related topic, boys will have more to include in their individual writing and be more confident to get started with a writing assignment.

- Encourage boys to draw their stories before writing (using graphics and storyboards). When given this opportunity, the quality and quantity of what boys produce increase dramatically.

- Use myths, storytelling, science fiction, and drama to help boys develop their imaginative skills and words for writing.

> - Paraphrase what boys say and have them repeat the revised message back to you using some of the new language you have shared, thus helping them improve their vocabulary for writing.

Dealing With Bias Toward and Censorship of Boys' Writing

Boys often feel censored by their teachers as they write on topics that interest them. Often, violence interests them, but they also live in a culture that has witnessed the price of violence and war, specifically on school grounds. Our culture is unsure of what to do with male aggression in general. In terms of boys' writing, teachers wonder where to draw the line between keeping writing appropriate and safe while still allowing boys to express their interests about topics of aggression that are central to their development as males, especially as they go through puberty.

In his book, *Boy Writers—Reclaiming Their Voices,* Ralph Fletcher states that he believes "violent writing is actually important to [boys'] development." He gives three reasons for allowing boys more choice and latitude in incorporating violence into their writing at school:

- A wider zone of engagement—the boys will be more interested in their writing and in the (writing) class as a whole when they see that they can bring their passions into it.

- Through written language they can safely grapple with power and danger, issues that make up a big part of a boys' internal world.

- Social capital—violent writing is classroom currency that can be "spent" and used to bond with friends.

Fletcher also states that "choice is negotiated between students and teacher, and this negotiation should take into account that there's a built-in culture (and gender) clash between the student's world and the world of the teacher. There must be common sense limitations on how much violence we permit in student writing." Undoubtedly, teachers will at times need to draw the line on what is appropriate. Boys can be very creative in their writing and some will use writing as an opportunity to express themselves in ways that are uncomfortable for teachers and for some of their classmates. Fletcher believes that boys should not be permitted to write in ways that are offensive, but he also knows that telling boys they can't write about certain topics may result in them simply writing more secretively about these topics.

In boys-only classes, there can be a certain freedom to deal with "dangerous" topics that, to a group of boys, may not feel too dangerous. Often, teachers in these classrooms compel boys to specify, at the top of the page, exactly what audience they are writing for. Their work needs to be appropriate for the audience for which it is intended. This will mean that some pieces may not include traces of violence but others can. This type of compromise is recognized as fair by most boys, and they appreciate the reasoning behind it and the opportunity to express themselves more freely on some occasions.

"Something very cool happened in my boy class today. We have been preparing for several days to write a historical fiction piece. With this piece we are focusing on writing about facts we have learned about Asheville history, adding dialogue, practicing correct punctuation, and including the elements of the writing process. The boys have been brainstorming and doing other pre-writing exercises in preparation for beginning their first draft today. Last Friday, when I reminded the boys that we would start writing on Monday, they said they were worried about their ability to write this three-page paper. I reminded them of the pre-writing and how to make that work for them. So today, remembering the concern I had witnessed on Friday, I came to class with some containers of paint. I told the boys we were going into the computer lab as warriors ready to conquer the white page. When they realized what we were doing, the boys got very excited. They lined up and actually giggled as I put war paint on their faces. They ran to the lab with their pre-writing in hand and started to write. As they typed, I made my way around the lab, conferencing with each one of them. When a boy finished a page, he stood on his chair, beat his chest, and shouted, 'I finished a page!' I have never had boys concentrate and accomplish as much as they did today. One boy finished almost two pages in one period. Yeah!!!"

—Bebe Zazzaro, Carolina Day School

Helping Boys Write Poetry

Poetry can inspire boys, but few boys spend much time reading or writing poetry, perhaps believing it is a particularly feminized form of writing. Considering that boys often struggle to find the words they need for writing, and that poetry uses fewer words and often a more fluid structure, perhaps we should increase our efforts to engage our boys in poetry. Once they see that poetry can be fun, and even mischievous—not necessarily romantic at all—boys may be more willing to give it a try. Boys often discover that poetry can be a way to express their feelings and emotions that might be too uncomfortable in another format.

One type of poem that boys seem to especially like writing are cinquains. Despite its French name, the *cinquain* is an American poetry form, developed and used to express brief thoughts and statements. Though the form does not have the extensive popularity of haiku, it is often taught in public schools to children because of its brief nature. Most cinquain poems consist of a single, twenty-two-syllable stanza, but they can be combined into longer works. A cinquain consists of five lines. The first line has two syllables, the second line has four syllables, the third line has six syllables, the fourth line has eight syllables, the final line has two syllables. The following examples were written by middle school boys.

Opening Game
Game time
Season looked good
National champions
We told ourselves as we sat down
Not now

Pickle
Pickle
Bumpy, Lumpy
Crunching, Munching, Lunching
Cucumbers making me pucker
Gherkin

Another style of poetry that teachers have found works well with boys is the *diamante*. A diamante is a seven-line poem, shaped like a diamond. The poem is structured as follows:

Line 1: one word (subject; noun) that is contrasting to line 7

Line 2: two words (adjectives) that describe line 1

Line 3: three words (action verbs) that relate to line 1

Line 4: four words (nouns), first two words relate to line 1, last two words relate to line 7

Line 5: three words (action verbs) that relate to line 7

Line 6: two words (adjectives) that describe line 7

Line 7: one word (subject; noun) that is contrasting to line 1

Here are a couple of fun examples of diamantes that were written during teacher training with the East Irondequoit School District in Rochester, New York. They relate to male-female brain differences and were used as an assessment exercise to see what participants had learned. The first one follows the format defined above while the second shows some "creativity." You can use this same activity in your classroom in any content area!

> Girls
> Verbal multi-task
> Bratty catty chatty
> Emotional-support change love guidance
> Rest risky move
> Task-oriented spatial
> Boys
>
>
> Adolescents
> Boys   Girls
> Work   in   progress
> Brains   continue   to   grow
> Adjust   your   expectations
> Be   patient
> Pray

At the beginning of each school year, an eighth-grade English teacher at a boys' school in Texas has her students write a diamante "describing themselves." After they complete the poem, she lets them use a graphics program on the computer to create a visual to accompany the poem that she hangs in the classroom for the semester. The boys love using a variety of fonts and some graphics to represent the flavor of the words they use to describe themselves. Before the end of school, she lets them redo the poem if they believe "who they are" is different from "who they were."

"The boys tend to know themselves pretty well and, surprisingly, they are quite honest in describing themselves in their poems. Almost all the students end up creating a new poem before the last day of school." Here's an example of a submission by a boy during the first weeks of school:

Lazy Funny
Swimming Singing Sleeping
Superman Champion Astronaut
Chillin' Studyin' Contemplatin'
Boring Quiet
Robert

Spencer Edmunds, middle school director at Canterbury School, has taught creative writing to boys and girls for many years. He says, "This involves tapping the creative ideas inside boys' brains and giving them the confidence and the courage to write with honesty, power and emotion. Getting girls to express themselves is much easier work." Along the way, he has had some successes with boys. He got one idea while working with the school's art department.

One day they observed an artist who took mundane objects (metal saw blades, wooden handles, and so on) and painted them artistically. Spencer decided to take that concept into his writing classroom, where instead of saw blades he used balls. Spencer says, "I purchased an assortment of cheap balls (footballs, basketballs, bouncy play balls), and had the students compose poems which they would

actually put directly on the balls. They wrote their final versions directly on the balls with permanent pens. There was a math element too, as we calculated how to make the space on the ball work for the number of lines of poetry. In the end, we came out with a really cool assortment of poetry balls. While I did this with both boys and girls, the boys really enjoyed this project."

A number of other teachers have told us how important the boys in their classrooms have found poems to be while they are going through difficult times. Here is one example that speaks loudly to a boy's emotions:

Blinded

Blinded by the surprise
Of two people's sorrow
I look into their eyes
And say, "Explain to me, explain to me
Why?"

The father bird has left the nest seeking a new life
It's sad, dark, and sorrowful
I sit there in the middle of nowhere
Just thinking what to do
It's like a constant battle
Like the war in Iraq

I can't do anything, I can't make them stop
I'm lost, what do I do?

They taught me about Santa Claus
They taught me how to tie my shoes
Together they are one
And now they are like a separated worm

Lonesome in the dark cellar she sits and waits to see
If he will return to the nest

—A 6th grade boy

Finding Their Words Through Journaling

Journals are a place where boys can reflect on personal experiences, think about memories, and write personal stories. Many teachers notice that boys think of journals as diaries, which they regard as a more girl-friendly activity. To help with this, teachers at Carolina Day have encouraged boys to call their writing books by more boy-friendly names. Since that time, boys have found it easier to write in their "Captain's Log" or "Pirate's Journal." One boys' class decided to call their journals "Bobs."

When one teacher noticed that her boys' class was not writing as much as she knew they could in their journal entries, she suggested that the boys count the words in their next journal entry and write the number at the end of the entry. Just adding this small suggestion of competition (no reward promised), caused the boys to nearly double the length of their entries.

Journals can serve several purposes in the classroom, and teachers should carefully explain how assigned journal writing will be used. Students should always know when writing is private and when it will be read. If the journal is assigned for private reflection and writing, students may at times still want the option of sharing certain entries with a teacher or classmates. Some high school and college students use online journaling to communicate with other students in some of their challenging classes, sharing their observations, understandings, and difficulties. Journaling about what they are learning in class is a great way to get students thinking more about what they learn and how they learn.

When boys journal, they often share their humor, adding cartoons and drawings to represent their ideas. They write about what is most present in their thinking. When boys feel the need, they will use their journals to speak about their feelings and their concerns. This confirms that boys are working to manage their emotional lives and that they enjoy finding comfortable avenues to express their feelings. This serves a great purpose for boys, as these expressions might not occur in any other ways. It is always interesting when a boy chooses to share a journal entry that speaks to his thoughts on life and growing up.

"Sometimes in my life, I wish there was just a place where I could go and hide and get away from the world. Everything can come at you so fast.

You can kind of lose track of the fact that you only get to live once. While something as seemingly meaningless as walking a little slower to enjoy the day, or just sitting in the grass perfectly quiet, can seem tedious, it's a great opportunity to really look at yourself.

Everybody, including myself, is self-conscious, always caring what other people think about them. Almost everybody is guilty of doing this, but there is really no reason. People want to look good so other people will like them or so that they can have a little self-confidence. In a perfect world, nobody would care what you looked like, what clothes you wore, or how much money your family has. But of course, the world isn't perfect . . ."

Finding Their Words Through Storytelling

As part of a storytelling unit in social studies, sixth-grade boys at Carolina Day learned about the art of story writing and storytelling, especially as it related to the oral history of the Appalachian Mountains in western North Carolina. They learned about the elements of a good story and then crafted their own. They put the main events of their story on an index card with a symbol on the card that represented their story, and attached each boy's card to a "talking stick." Then the boys and their teacher, Ms. Zazzaro, took their stories outdoors. Sitting in a circle, each boy was called to tell his story with the following rhythm chant (while boys drum on the ground with their hands and with the talking stick):

"Brother, we have come to hear your story."

"Brother Jim, we want to hear your tale."

"Brother Jim, tell your story. . ."

The talking stick is passed to Jim, and eventually to each boy in the circle. Each boy uses his index card to remind him of the order of events in his story. In this situation, Ms. Zazzaro did not tell the boys to make eye contact, but they listened carefully and respectfully to the storyteller. As they listened, the boys began to build small houses from the sticks and pine needles on the ground. When all the stories were told, they realized they had created a small village, and they talked about the people who might have lived in their village—creating another story.

For a couple of weeks, the boys returned to the site to see if their village was still intact. The village survived a small dusting of snow, but was eventually washed away with the rain. The talking stick exercise was a meaningful experience that helped the boys use their words for speaking.

ENGAGING BOYS IN SOCIAL STUDIES

Social studies is a crucial area of focus that does not get as much attention as reading and writing in boys' curricula. A number of boys-only classrooms are innovating beautifully in social studies, and their activities also work for girls. More on girls' social studies innovations appears in the next chapter.

Dru Alexander's seventh-grade boys enjoy a unit she designed on the elements of Native American creation mythology. She introduces the unit by reading the *Navajo Origin Legend* by A.M. Stephen and *When Grizzlies Walked Upright* (a Modoc legend) to the entire class. Then the boys work in groups, reading and comparing a variety of myths, looking for common elements, and putting their findings on the board. The class also discusses how fetishes and totems relate to creation mythology.

To further their study, Dru reads Stephen Vincent Benet's *By the Waters of Babylon* to the boys. As they listen to the story, the boys are instructed to find ideas that they can later incorporate into their own myth developed around the story's protagonist. As they write these original myths, they also design an appropriate fetish or totem to use when they tell their story to the class.

Finally, on story day, the boys sit around a pretend campfire made with logs, colorful tissue paper, and a flashlight burning in the center to create the light of the fire. The room lights are turned off, and each boy enjoys the opportunity to share his myth.

Building a State

Beverly Rollins Edwards, a third-grade teacher at Greensboro Day School submitted the following social studies activity:

> As part of our social studies curriculum, we study North Carolina, its three regions and its topography. This year I have consciously tried to include more movement in my daily teaching, so I asked the kids if they wanted to "build North Carolina." They were, of course, very enthusiastic.
>
> I told one-third of my students to be the coastal plains. We talked about what they knew about the topography of the coastal plains. They wanted to show the beaches and how the land gradually rises toward the Piedmont. They positioned themselves on the floor and made their bodies as flat as possible. They stretched their hands out in front of them so that their fingers would be the sandy beaches that touch the Atlantic. The Piedmont region needed to be a bit bigger in size so I had more students in this group. They also lay flat on the floor, except they put their fingertips on the floor so that their hands were slightly raised to represent the fall line where the Piedmont meets the Coastal Plains. The Mountain group was the smallest in number, but the most excited. They talked about how to represent the mountains and decided to get on their knees and joined their hands in upside-down V's to make the peaks. It was spectacular. For the rest of the unit they remembered all the regions and the topography of each.

Silent Debates

Russell White from Crespi Carmelite High School has the boys in his social studies classes do **silent debates**. Students partner up and share one piece of blank paper for the debate. They debate a topic they have discussed in the classroom, such as the production of cash crops or the implementation of capitalism in developing nations. Each student is assigned a particular side of an argument or a specific point of view. The two students then debate the topic, on paper. No talking is allowed as one student records a statement about his topic and then passes the paper to his partner, who responds. This continues back and forth for an allotted amount of time. Then the boys submit their written silent debate. When time permits, the boys read their debates to the class.

All-Star Lineups

Seventh-grade boys in Dru Alexander and Chris McGrath's social studies classes at Carolina Day studied the Civil War and did a baseball card project. They created an **all-star lineup** of Civil War heroes with baseball cards, including "stats"

and quotations on the back of each card for famous or infamous generals and other officers. They also made "wildcards" with "field information" on various battlegrounds.

A Country Card

Russell White also created a **country card project**. This world history project requires each student to select two countries from two different continents. No students in the same class are allowed to use the same countries. Once the countries are selected, students research and make a series of six cards for each country, plus one bibliography card (total of thirteen cards). Students use appropriate Internet sites to research the countries and gather information for their cards. Students type up the cards and add an appropriate picture with a caption. As a follow-up, students share the most interesting information with their classmates and everyone has the opportunity to learn more about these countries. The following information must be placed on each card:

Card #1	Map of Country	Name of country; capital; major cities; key geographic features
Card #2	Currency	Name of currency; picture; recent exchange rate to U.S. dollar
Card #3	Government	Type; leader and title; date of independence and from whom
Card #4	Economy	Products produced; products exported; products imported
Card #5	Fun Facts	Something famous or interesting about the country
Card #6	History	A highlight; a lowlight

The Imperator

Tod Post, a Latin teacher from Crespi, sends the following activity called **Imperator,** which is Latin for emperor. As there are no Latin restaurants, radio stations, TV programs, or movies, Tod finds it difficult to infuse Latin culture into his teaching. So he invented Imperator to give his boys a better sense of what Rome was like. This activity can also be adapted to other curricular units to help students learn about social class.

All the boys in Latin I start out as slaves, working to become emperor, but only one can reach that level. Tod gives each of his boys an action figure. He sculpted the original action figure (11-in. tall) and made a mold from which he casts copies each year. Each boy paints his figure and picks an authentic Latin name for it. Of course, slaves only get one name (as opposed to the three names that citizens have).

One of the most popular activities in Imperator is the slave sale at the beginning of the year. After the Latin I students paint their new slaves and name them, they are sold into slavery to the Latin II–IV students who have earned currency to spend. This creates a situation in which the success of the upper-level students becomes partially dependent on the success of the lower-level students, so the upper-level students have a reason and motivation to help tutor their "slaves."

The main way that a slave can earn money is through vocabulary quizzes. For every word that a student gets correct on a quiz he earns one coin. For this game, Tod uses copies of Roman coins in eight different denominations, all based on real Roman currency, and the boys actually receive the money that they earn. Each boy works his way from slave to gladiator, then freeman, patrician, legionary,

centurion, senator, consul, and finally one becomes emperor. The levels are based on authentic Roman classes, offices, and the like.

In order to advance to the next level, students must earn honor points. They earn these primarily by learning certain skills or winning skill-based competitions. For example, to go from slave to gladiator a student must show that he has learned some basics about Latin nouns and verbs. The activities vary from level I Latin to level IV. Activities include quizzes, head-to-head competitions, building, writing, and speaking.

As a slave, a boy has no abilities or privileges. His goal is to earn honor for his master. As the students advance they earn more money and do more things, obtaining tools, weapons, buildings, and so forth. A freeman can own a shop and earn more money through his business. Consuls lead the army into war, senators get to create laws and tax the other citizens.

Boys keep the same action figure for the entire time they are in Latin class at Crespi, but as they advance they change the costumes, the armor, and the accessories that the figure wears. As a teacher, Tod enjoys finding opportunities to create, so this is a way for him to bring a little bit of art to a highly verbal subject. The competition motivates boys to learn tedious grammar and vocabulary lists. The characters provide a great opportunity to get high school boys to focus and write. Tod has found that if he asks boys to write in Latin about particular topics, he gets less than desirable results, but he says that if he asks them to write in Latin about their characters in given situations, his boys "can write and write."

One of the main reasons Tod's students enjoy the game so much is the element of competition. They all like to earn money and check the chart on the wall to see who is in first place. Many build things for their characters or come up with games that involve their characters. Tod says, "I find that many high school boys are more fascinated by Rome than by Latin (I happen to like both), so having a hands-on, visual presentation for Latin and Roman culture tends to hold their interest more than a purely verbal presentation of Latin."

Tod, like so many teachers, is constantly innovating to bring different elements of core curricula together—social studies meets languages meets math meets science. As the use of single-sex classes increases throughout the United States, it is probable that there will be a growing emphasis on integrating across curricula as Tod is doing, and this will be true for both boys and girls.

WRAPPING UP THE MAIN POINTS

When teachers innovate in boys-only classrooms toward core curricula success, we find that they generally include these elements:

- Lots of movement and hands-on, interactive learning experiences
- Less time "sitting and getting" and more time "doing"
- Opportunities for boys to work together, learning from each other's strengths
- Strategically planned transition times
- Healthy competition whenever possible and appropriate
- Boy-friendly content in language arts and social studies
- And remember to make sure students have access to water at all times

Strategies for Teaching Core Curricula to Girls

My calculus teacher makes the rules of calculus into songs for better memorization. She plays the accordion as the class sings.

—Olivia, 12th grade girl

In its Biennial Report to the United States Congress in 2002, the National Science Foundation reported that

> [A]lthough through fourth grade, equal numbers of girls and boys reported that they like science and math . . .
>
> - By eighth grade, girls' interest in math and confidence in their math abilities have eroded, even though they perform as well as boys in this subject
> - By eighth grade, twice as many boys as girls show an interest in science and engineering careers

- By high school, even girls with exceptional preparation in math and science are choosing careers in science and math in disproportionately low numbers

- Many girls don't picture themselves as future scientists or engineers. They don't put a female face on these professions because they rarely see real-life or media images of female scientists.

This report is one of many that point out an erosion of confidence for many girls in their ability to perform in core subjects in the math and science areas. As a result of their experiences in single-sex classrooms, girls often begin to consider the broader possibilities that are available to them, and can become more willing to pursue nontraditional girl options. Armed with the knowledge of how girls learn and what girls need, teachers can help many girls evaluate all their choices, based on their abilities and interests, and encourage them down challenging career paths. This chapter is devoted to helping you help the girls in your girls-only classroom. Many of the strategies in this chapter, like those throughout this book, can be adapted to a coed classroom. Some, however, will feel uniquely suitable to a girls-only environment.

HELPING GIRLS DO WELL IN MATHEMATICS

When girls succeed at a math lesson or on a math quiz, they attribute their success to luck; boys attribute it to their own inner ability. . . . That's why girls . . . don't develop the kind of confidence males do. Teen-age boys along with girls' parents send out many signals to girls that math is a male domain. Even boys who have difficulty with math stick it out because they believe it holds the key to careers they want. Girls are permitted to quit.

—Sheila Tobias

From as early as the upper elementary school grades, girls frequently say that they do not like math. This may be caused and is certainly reinforced by the messages they receive that "math is hard" and "math is more for boys"—messages that cause girls to doubt their ability, even though they may be making good grades. They start to become cautious about what math may be like for them in the future, often developing a fear of math. As educators work to remove the biases that suggest girls are poorer performers in math, women in particular need to be careful about using phrases such as, "I was never good at math."

In 1994, Teen Barbie announced "Math is hard. Let's go shopping." Mattel took some heat for promoting a negative stereotype about girls and math and as a result withdrew the doll from the market, but the fact that they issued this doll making this statement reflected a pervasive social attitude.

Increasing Spatial and Manipulative Learning

Boys tend to have superior spatial skills, and they grow up playing with building blocks and other toys that move and transform their shape. Girls tend to do less of this. They often prefer toys that allow them to play in a world more focused on relationships, paying less attention to toys that are more spatial or mechanical in design. An awareness of this child development difference is a starting point from which to change negative patterns in math learning for girls. Teachers who are conscious of this difference often notice right away that change can come when girls are presented with opportunities for spatial learning.

Using Spatial Techniques   A common and enjoyable way to connect math to spatial parts of the brain is to use a jump rope to practice math facts. You can take your girls outside and have them work in groups, jumping rope as they practice counting by 2s, or counting down from multiples of 9 (81, 72, 63, 54, 45, and so on), or doing their multiplication facts.

"I teach math [in single-sex classes] and the most noticeable change I have seen is how willing students [in single-sex classes] are to solve problems on the board. In past years I would have students REFUSE to go to the board to solve problems. This year I can't think of one student who refused to go to the board. In fact, in the girls' classes they are begging to go up! Even when they get the problem wrong, the other students will help them figure out where they made their mistake. There is no embarrassment or shame. It's a beautiful thing!"

—Julia Carlesso, Wolfe Middle School

Another popular activity in girls-only classrooms requires a larger space. To teach girls about addition and place value, find a large space and assign seven girls to stand in an area designated as the ones column with each girl representing "one." Put two girls in an adjacent area and tell the group that these girls represent "two tens" which together make twenty. Now ask the girls to determine what number they all represent when the ones and tens are added together (twenty-seven). Tell the girls you are going to add fourteen to this number and have them place remaining girls in the correct columns, assigning each a one or ten value as required. With eleven girls now in the ones column, girls should realize that ten of the ones must be exchanged for one ten. You can change numbers and work with place value in a number of ways, and use subtraction as well.

Using Manipulatives   Jim Roberts, a math teacher at Woodward Elementary, says "I use a lot of math manipulatives. In my single-sex classes I have learned that if girls' hands are doing what you want them to do, then their minds are too. Hands engaged equals brains engaged." Whenever Jim brings out manipulatives for math instruction in his girls-only class, he allows the girls to play with the items for a full minute or two, just so they get comfortable with the manipulatives before they need to use them. (With the boys, he gives them only a few seconds, knowing they will quickly see how they might be used and then proceed to invent other less constructive uses for them.)

The use of manipulatives—which is hands-on spatial tasking—helps girls experience math in the real world by seeing how things work; building objects and taking things apart; examining, measuring, comparing, and estimating. This triggers the brain to excite many areas of math learning that become necessary for complex math. It is useful to remember that math learning is not just numerical (counting); it is inherently spatial. Each math abstraction a student studies involves manipulation of spatial ideas and icons in the imagination. This is the kind of math learning that greater tactile and spatial learning can help with.

To learn more about math manipulatives, check out Montessori Web sites or go to a Montessori school in your area; the Montessori method includes a great deal of emphasis on tactile and spatial learning for math.

"I love having my sixth- and seventh-grade boys and girls in separate math classes this year. The classes are really different in terms of personality, and I think these students are much more comfortable being themselves in the given setting. The girls are more involved than they were last year in coed classes. I really, really like the separation, and I wish I had it in my eighth grade too."

—Robin van Alstyne, enriched math teacher

Encouraging Risk Taking

Middle school math teacher Joe Kirstein sees that boys are bigger risk takers in his single-sex math classes, willing to dig in to understand a concept. The girls usually prefer having a defined procedure, working from their notes to follow specific steps. Girls are good at applying this method assiduously, but often do not risk making enough mistakes to obtain generalized meaning from the particular lesson, and therefore fail to grasp the depth of what they are learning. This means that at some point, when somewhat similar problems show up, girls may recognize the situations and know that they have solved similar problems, but may not be able to repeat the process without some reteaching.

Math teachers in all settings have noticed that girls often need to be encouraged to practice taking more risks in math. This requires an attitude change, and it is one that many girls-only classrooms can address immediately, without interference from boys.

Many of the activities in the following section can help you engage girls in more risk taking.

"Recently in math class as we were going around the room checking our work, the girls began to preface their answers with phrases like "I don't think this is right but . . ." or "I'm not sure I did this right, but . . ." It was really surprising to me that the girls should have such little confidence in their work, even though most of their answers were correct. I made a rule that they were only allowed to state their answer without commentary. I'm not sure where the lack of confidence comes from . . . it certainly isn't based on their actual performance in math class!"

—Karla Weidner, 6th grade math teacher

Math Activities That Work

A number of teachers in girls-only classes have reported innovating along sensorial lines to increase girls' math learning and math facts memorization. These teachers have observed that many girls do well with sensory data, noticing and remembering colors with great variety. These teachers have constructed some of their math instruction via multisensory techniques, such as by using multicolored categories. They invite the girls to do multiplication numbers in red, division numbers in green, and so on. This helps utilize sensorial parts of the female brain in math learning. Most of the following activities can include, should you wish them to, a direct conversation with girls about sensorial categories, colors, textures, and shapes that they may associate with each piece of math learning.

Coordinates Tools   Middle school math teacher Crystal Fowler uses a movement activity called **Simon Says Coordinate Grids** to review the four quadrants, origin, and x and y axis. Crystal says,

> I teach girls the related vocabulary and then show them how to act out each word in the game. The following terms are taught using the corresponding motion:
>
> Quadrant I—students point above their heads with both hands to the right
>
> Quadrant II—students point above their heads with both hands to the left
>
> Quadrant III—students point to the ground with both hands to the left
>
> Quadrant IV—students point to the ground with both hands to the right
>
> Origin—students hold their stomachs with both hands
>
> Y axis—students move both hands up and down in front of their bodies
>
> X axis—students move both hands horizontally in front of their bodies
>
> I play along with them during the first game with my back to them and act out each motion. For example, if I say "Simon says origin," the girls should put their hands on their stomachs. After they have practiced the game, I face them and call out terms such as "quadrant I" and watch how they move and if they move. If they move when I did not say "Simon says" or if they use the incorrect motion for the term, they are out and must sit down. Those who are out watch and check to see if the others are correct.

After my students master these motions, I sometimes add in things like "positive-positive" to see if they know which quadrant has those values. In this case they should be pointing to quadrant I (above their heads to the right). We play several rounds of Simon Says and the winners receive a small reward. This activity is a fun way to teach the vocabulary. Later, when my girls take MAP tests or other classroom assessments, I can see them acting out the grid at their desk to remember the vocabulary and apply their skills.

Dr. Ross, the middle school principal at Stratford Academy in Macon, Georgia, and a former math teacher, confirms the usefulness of this kind of project. He turns the classroom into a coordinate plane by allowing girls to set it up by numbering desks on an X-Y grid, then providing each girl with a different card on which are written coordinates such as (2, −3). The girls then find the appropriate desks from the coordinates. A card under the desk tells them if they have been successful. At times he hides an object at a particular coordinate to create additional interest. According to Dr. Ross, this activity, and the fact that the girls help to set it up, facilitates their understanding of the coordinate plane. He also uses a blank coordinate plane on a SMART board as a model for instruction.

Single Hands Math   To warm up her third graders for math, Rachael Ide has them turn to their math partner and play **Single Hands Math**; one partner is labeled "A" and the other "B." Students will either add, subtract, or multiply the numbers they choose to display with their fingers. The students take turns answering their math problems. For example, Student A displays five fingers on the desk and her partner, Student B, displays four fingers. Then the teacher tells all groups that A students should multiply ($5 \times 4 = 20$). Next time the B students solve the problem. Later in the year, they begin playing **Double Hands Math**, using both hands for bigger numbers. This is a clear example of an innovation that utilizes, among other things, girls' natural sensorial apprehensions and abilities.

Math Relays and Concentration Math   Karla Weidner finds that this kind of competitive learning can inspire the girls to take risks. She shared these tools with us:

> I take my sixth-grade girls outside for **math relays**. I divide them into teams of three to four players and have them line up about twenty feet from where I am standing. On my start, each team sends player 1 to me to pick up a copy of a math problem (I use challenging problems for this team activity). She then returns to her teammates and the team works together to quickly solve the problem. Once they think they have the correct answer, player 2 runs to me to show me their answer. If correct, they get a new problem. If wrong, player 2 returns to her team so they can redo the first problem. Players take turns running to me with their team's answer, hoping to also pick up the next problem. The teams have several problems to solve together, and the first team to successfully finish all the problems correctly is the winner.

Karla also has her girls play **Concentration Math** to review math concepts. She places cards with math problems and cards with the solutions around the classroom in various places (high, low, underneath things). Individually the girls find problems and their matching solutions. The goal of the game is for each girl to find as many matches as she can in a certain period of time. The girls have to show the problem card and its corresponding solution card to Karla before they can claim the match. If they are wrong, they must replace the pieces so others can use them. This combination of sensorial learning and risk taking increases the effectiveness of math learning for her girls.

Using Brain Gym During Lessons   According to fifth-grade math teacher Kim Broshar, "Teaching long division is one of the most tedious and difficult concepts of the year. Since I began using Brain Gym activities while introducing the concepts, I've seen a big learning difference." (See more about Brain Gym in Chapter Five). Kim uses the Brain Gym activities as needed—usually when she notices her girls' brows furrow or a glazed-over look comes into their eyes. She stops the lesson and inserts a quick activity. Kim provides examples: "We use 'gravity gliders,' 'neck rolls,' or 'lazy eights.' I've found that just taking the break is helpful in itself, but even more, engaging the brain in brain gymnastics allows the girls to refocus, while providing the settling time needed to comprehend the new concept."

Before she started using Brain Gym to help students calm and refocus for math, Kim noticed that her girls were frequently frustrated to the point of tears. This is not the case anymore. She adds, "Using Brain Gym activities as I teach long division has made this whole process easier for girls. They comprehend long division quicker and their retention of the information is stronger for follow up activities and independent practice."

Imaginative Learning   Math learning can often be enhanced by engaging imaginative parts of the brain. So much of math is abstract learning that it utilizes some of the same regions of the cerebral cortex that imagination and fantasy utilize. Eighth-grade math teacher Crystal Fowler utilizes this connection via a reward system called **Fantasy Vacation**. It encourages friendly competition in her girls-only classroom while engaging girls' imaginations regarding where they would like to go on vacation, and how much that vacation will cost.

Crystal says,

> First, I teach decimal rules, including the importance of lining up decimals when adding or subtracting. We also discuss the importance of managing money and how to balance and maintain a checkbook. The girls make their own checkbook using copies of blank checks and blank registers. We hang these on a chart at the back of the room. Each week they can earn money and lose money based on their attendance, behavior, and completion of homework assignments, by debiting or crediting their account.
>
> Ultimately, they are earning money for a fantasy vacation, so they need to equalize the debit and credit amounts to vacations they can purchase when they save enough money. Each week on Monday, the girls debit and credit their accounts based on the information collected from the previous week. When they earn enough money for a certain vacation, they write me a check for the amount of the vacation. I review their account records and distribute their rewards. Vacation packages change, but possible vacation sites include New York, Europe and Hawaii. More expensive vacations provide more rewards, but they take longer to purchase. Sample rewards are homework passes, snacks and free time.

Crystal adds, "This imaginative but very concrete game has proven to be a great incentive for my girls. Each week they are so excited about working on their checkbooks that they forget they are also completing a math assignment."

Incorporate Girls' Verbal Skills

Many girls' math teachers around the country have found it immensely helpful to involve girls' verbal skills as much as possible in math learning. As much as you can, let girls talk with one another about the problems they are solving. They will often solve problems verbally with one another. And because verbal skills also include writing, assigning a journal activity can enhance math learning. Sometimes it can be helpful to give girls prompts for writing about their daily lessons. Some suggestions include:

- Today I learned . . .
- I saw a pattern for . . .
- My participation today . . .
- I was surprised that I . . .
- I did not understand . . .
- The most important thing to remember about our problems today . . .
- We did something fun . . .
- It was easy to grasp . . .
- Here is a drawing I created to illustrate a math problem today . . .
- I made a connection . . .
- Two different ways to solve this problem are . . .
- When math is hard, I . . .
- I have a new strategy for . . .
- I estimated (or predicted) . . .

Incorporate Music into Math Learning

Throughout human history, music has helped children learn. Many of the same parts of the brain used for math are also used for music. You can make music work for girls by teaching mnemonic devices, chants, or rhymes to help them remember important math concepts, operations, or vocabulary. If you let girls make up their own musical accompaniments, this can add to the learning.

In some schools, girls are encouraged to bring in sunglasses and hats to set the mood as they create and perform **math raps**, showing their knowledge of specific math topics. Here is an example of a math rap that appears in *Celebrating Multiple Intelligences: Teaching for Success* (used with permission of New City School).

Place Value Rap
The number of digits in our system is ten,
You will learn their value if you just begin.
There's a zero, there's a one, two, three, four,
five, six, seven, eight, nine, no more.
Every digit has a value on its face;
and each digit has a value in its place.
Two can be two ones or two can be two tens.
Either way it's two, the value just depends
On where you put it,
On where you put it.
The value just depends on where you put it.
Two tens are twenty and two ones are two.
When you use the proper place it's easy to do.

[Repeat]

That's a rap!

TRY THIS: Make Math Relevant and Fun for Girls

Here is a checklist of activities of relevant math activities you can put to use right away in your classes. Each targets a connection for girls between their identity, their real lives, and math learning.

- Find out what activities girls in your class are involved in, and incorporate math problems that speak to those interests.
- Play games in math, especially as a review before a test. Divide into teams and make it competitive for girls. Math Jeopardy and Math Baseball are

---

good examples. Life is competitive, and competition in math can feel like real life.

- Get girls out of their desks and working problems on the board. This is a great way for teachers to see how well they understand a concept, and it can make math more active and less passive.

- Give homework assignments that do not always involve a worksheet or a textbook. Ask girls to gather math information at home (such as identifying shapes or angles in the design of their house) to use in class the next day.

- Set a classroom timer for three minutes. Then ask girls to share the ways that math is used in their daily lives. They should have many examples, such as calculating tips, balancing checkbooks, measuring recipe amounts, scheduling events on a calendar, buying groceries, managing their time with homework, buying lunches, getting to class on time, and so on.

HELPING GIRLS LEARN SCIENCE

By nature, science learning begins in the parts of the brain that govern spatial and abstract learning. Success in science requires experimentation—the willingness to take risks. Not surprisingly, then, it initially presents girls with many of the same challenges they face in math, regardless of their ages. Here are two illustrative examples.

Lower school science specialist at Greensboro Day School, Rose Marie Cook, uses LEGO® blocks in the science lab to teach about simple machines to her fourth-grade students. She noticed that girls tend to look at the directions and follow them, touching only the necessary pieces, all the time using supportive tones with each other. The boys tend to just glance at the directions. They skip steps that they see as unnecessary, grab pieces and stick them together, even when it isn't their turn to build. The boys also tend to create their own unique machines, all the time humming and making all kinds of "mechanical" sound effects. The girls tend to work more quietly.

According to Rose Marie,

> "Not only is the building process very different, but the machines themselves are usually very interesting. One example that comes to mind was "the fan." The girls made the fan exactly as the directions stated. When asked how it might be used, they said that it would be used to cool their family off on a hot summer day. The boys, on the other hand, got their fan constructed in about the same time frame, even though they had to start over three times. When asked how it would be used, they instantly attached the LEGO people to the paddles and made them spin so fast that they flew off. Then, one of the boys said, "Look, if this one gets too close, it might cut his head off!"

A second example was recalled by John Douglas, middle school assistant principal:

> As part of the eighth grade science curriculum, we ask students to build motorized, programmable LEGO cars. The students use software to write computer programs that make the cars perform various tasks such as going prescribed distances, backing up, spinning in circles, and playing music. The students are grouped in pairs and given all the LEGO equipment and instructions on how to program their cars.
>
> I've noticed that after I go over general directions and pass out the materials, all of the boy groups start digging around in the boxes and slapping LEGO pieces together. Every girl group first finds the instructions, looks at the diagrams, and then starts to build their vehicles by using the diagrams as models. Over the two weeks that we work on this project, the boy groups continually experiment with design using a trial and error method. The girl groups study the instructions and also go around the room to observe what other groups are doing.
>
> At the end of the unit, all groups have successfully completed the tasks that were given to them, but they have used totally different methods.

These examples of science learning differences do not show an inferiority in the more orderly, lower-risk method girls often use. It does show, however, a primary reason many girls may not choose scientific careers later in life: their sense of

scientific inquiry and risk taking did not develop as quickly and confidently as the boys' might have, and as the boys become men, they take into their adult careers a greater variety of early science learning, especially a sense of experimentation that will later create success in science.

Helping Girls Gain Scientific Confidence from Elementary to Secondary Levels

To help girls gain early confidence in scientific inquiry and method, teachers in girls-only science classes often concentrate on keeping girls' natural curiosity for science high. Rote learning often does not lead to much deep understanding, so in order to engage girls more deeply, teachers use discussion regarding how a scientific principle relates to girls' real lives.

Elementary school teachers also report gaining ground by teaching to the natural strengths and interests of young girls. They ask the girls what they are interested in, and work with them to turn that interest area—soccer or music or relationships—into science learning. They also integrate lots of "verbal or talk time" into science lessons.

As she began teaching science in her single-sex class, Deborah Roberts of Woodward Elementary realized that her girls like talking about people—not about how things work in the world. They struggled with physical science because it often did not interest them. This was evident from the 2005–2006 scores on the Florida science assessment test: only 24 percent of the fifth-grade girls passed as compared to 53 percent of the fifth-grade boys.

Deborah knew she needed to make some fundamental changes in terms of the way the girls were perceiving physical science—changes that would make this subject more appealing to them. She realized that the science book they were using began each unit with a discovery-based activity. Previously, she had noticed that boys dug in and enjoyed this type of challenge, but many of the girls were struggling with it right from the beginning of each chapter.

In 2006–2007, she began a new approach for the girls. Recognizing that her girls' strengths lie more in verbal skills than spatial skills, she began each science unit guiding them through two textbook lessons and a related technology lesson to build background knowledge. Only then did they attempt the discovery activity. As a result, the girls have been more interested and less reticent to get involved with science.

By the middle school years, girls-only science teachers help girls gain access to female role models among scientists. The classroom has more than a few visitors every year, from the female scientific and medical community. Often relatives or family friends of the girls will come into class and lead a lesson or speak.

Many teachers have also told us that girls seem to take a special interest in real problems faced in small and large communities, locally and globally. Group projects are often valuable ways to involve the girls in real-world issues such as pollution studies or poverty issues.

Visual mechanisms often catalyze girls as well—especially regarding the brain. Some teachers in single-sex classes have found their students to be especially fascinated by the human sciences, and can often go onto the Internet and download brain scans that girls find fascinating. Creating costumes to represent parts of a cell and then having a "cell fashion show" made a biology lesson more engaging for these girls!

In each case, when a girl's fascination is piqued, whether by a tool, a speaker, or a social issue, the teacher soon exposes the girls to science-related disciplines that can help promote solutions to real-world problems in, for example, neuroscience, astronomy, computer science, oncology, and environmental sciences.

By the time girls reach high school, they can find great interest and self-confidence in research programs, including internships and shadowing experiences that partner girls with professional mentors and scientists who do cutting-edge research. For young women, recent research has shown mentoring in science to be one of the key factors in later science success.

Whenever possible, you can take your girls to research labs where they can meet people who will show them how research is conducted. If possible, help girls attend science- and technology-related conferences. In order not to lose a single girl who shows interest in science majors, it may be important for science teachers to help each girl find the appropriate colleges and universities for science- and technology-based careers.

From elementary school through high school (and well into college), many girls need extra help from mentors and teachers to move confidently into careers in science.

The National Girls Collaborative Project awards mini-grants to programs designed especially for girls in science, technology, engineering, and mathematics (STEM) to support collaboration, address gaps and overlaps in service, and share promising practices. In a number of states, there are projects designed to build collaboration between existing programs and organizations in order to encourage girls to pursue STEM-related educational programs and careers. For more information on developing a collaborative project for your school community, visit the Web site: www.psctlt.org/ngcp/index.html.

HELPING GIRLS GAIN TECHNOLOGICAL CONFIDENCE

In a study entitled "How Adolescent Boys and Girls View Today's Computer Culture," Dr. Alice A. Christie, associate professor of technology and education and graduate studies department chair at Arizona State University West, used

observations and focus groups to find out how girls and boys defined computers and used computers. She states, "The gender differences surrounding technology are not differences in competence, confidence, or frequency of use. Instead, the differences lie in how adolescent girls and boys view computers and the way they choose to use them." (Examples below used with permission of Dr. Christie.)

Girls' Definitions

- Something to keep you connected to your friends.
- It helps you communicate with others.
- A tool that does things that you tell it to do.
- A lot of stuff combined into one thing to make life easier.
- A gateway to information.
- It can substitute for a book because it contains so much information.
- It organizes and stores your thoughts.
- It's a resource tool for learning things.
- It can communicate, it can do problems in math, and it can write.
- It improves your everyday life.
- A tool that makes your work look neater and more professional.
- A tool that helps you work quicker.
- It's whatever you want it to be.

Boys' Definitions

- A machine with a CPU and a motherboard and circuits.
- A high-tech calculator, a giant calculator.
- A machine that does what you program it to do.
- A machine that thinks for you.
- A machine that processes information and stores it.
- A toy for people to have for entertainment.
- A machine that does things faster than a human can.

- A machine that allows you to look up stuff.
- It lets you do things more quickly and easily.

Dr. Christie's study shed light also on boys' and girls' daily uses of the computer.

Girls' Uses of Computers

- Word processing for homework and research
- Word processing for writing process to easily do lots of drafts
- PowerPoint presentations for classes
- E-mail to talk to friends both locally and at a distance
- Chat rooms to keep in touch with friends and make new friends
- Instant messaging to talk to classmates
- E-mail to talk to guys and flirt with guys
- Games to play if I'm really, really bored, like PacMan or Solitaire
- Definitely NOT for games
- The Internet to shop or "window shop"

Boys' Uses of Computers

- Mainly for fun, maybe some homework now and then
- To play games (Solitaire, casino games, sporting games, logic games, simulations where you kill people, war games)
- Entertainment twenty-four hours a day
- The Internet for information to do homework
- The Internet for Nintendo codes
- Run an FTP from my computer that's up twenty-four hours a day

Among the many fascinating findings in this study, you may have noticed, is how much boys associate computers with fun. From very early on, boys associate learning with the physical objects they play with, far more than they do with the words used around them. Developing their verbal skills later than girls, and inclined especially in the early years toward more spatial and kinesthetic learning, boys gravitate toward projects that provide spatial fun (physical games) and learn via physical tools.

Computers are a physical and virtual version of both a spatial object (virtual space) and physical tool (filled with virtual tools). As tool users and spatial thinkers, boys will tend to spend more time exercising their mental muscles among the wide variety of tools, objects, symbols, and games in a computer.

Though girls spend a great deal of computer time on the Internet chatting and e-mailing friends, the "fun" of the computer comes in the relationship building and the "function" of the computer comes in the homework and writing enhancement. Girls do not spend as much time as boys do understanding the wide variety of technological uses, nor the technology itself.

As our economy becomes more computer oriented, girls are challenged to compensate for this gap, and teachers of girls find themselves challenged to creatively and clearly help girls gain "fun and function" from the range of available computer technologies around them. This means engaging girls in computer design rather than just computer use. Putting girls in single-sex computer classes—where they are not overwhelmed by the technology skills of boys— can often be a first step toward engaging girls in the full use of the computer. Removing the boys can sometimes make computer technology more fun and exciting.

TRY THIS: Actively Involve Girls in Integrated Science (Including Math and Technology)

Math, science, and computer technology are often overlapping subjects in school, and are sometimes taught by the same teachers. If a girl has an issue of confidence in one of these three classes, she may have a similar issue in another one. For this reason, we have created this checklist of solutions and activities that integrate all three kinds of learning. These come from teachers like you who teach these topics.

- **Teach girls about tools**. Find ways to let girls change a tire, fix a leaky faucet, repair a bicycle, replace a part, hook up a DVD player.

- Ask girls to **design and build bird houses**. Have them research styles of bird houses that will work for specific birds that live in their community, make drawings and cardboard models of the houses they will build, decide on the materials (size and amount) to be purchased, learn to use the appropriate tools safely, and finally build and install the houses. This project will encourage risk taking and build confidence in girls.

- Give girls spatial activities and **assignments without the use of written instructions**. Provide girls with materials and ask them to build structures for specific purposes without models or assistance, encouraging them to use their reasoning and problem-solving skills to produce a product. In the process, they will gain confidence from what they were able to achieve on their own.

- Have girls partner with girls of the same age in other schools to **read and discuss books through e-mail**. Be sure to select high-interest books with strong female characters. Guide the girls to discuss critically what they read and to analyze the characters and their actions in the books. This activity gets girls more involved in using technology while promoting their interests in reading and developing relationships.

- Ask girls to design a project-based learning activity related to **women in science**, involving research and employing technology. Encourage applications to real-world situations, perhaps the availability of science careers for women.

- Design a role-playing exercise for girls in which **each girl assumes the role of a notable female scientist**. Have each girl select and research a scientist, learning as much as possible about her education, her work, and her successes in a particular field. Then host a summit meeting with the girls playing their parts and speaking in the voices of their female scientists. Let the topic of the summit be "Encouraging Young Women to Pursue Science as a Career." Consider asking one or two local female scientists from a nearby college or university to participate in the summit.

- Have someone who works in computer technology speak in the class about how computers work, **both hardware and software**.

- **Ask a female speaker** to come to the computer class and discuss how she got involved in a career in computer technology.

HELPING GIRLS EXCEL IN LANGUAGE ARTS

Compared to boys, girls have been much more successful in the areas of reading and writing, meeting—to a greater degree—the expectations of their teachers. On average, girls spend more time reading than boys and are often better able to translate their thoughts into writing. Girls often enjoy writing and especially like using it to express themselves in ways they may not do in classroom conversation. They are generally more patient with the whole writing process than many boys are, and more willing to persevere to improve a piece of writing. Given that writing is enhanced (and receives a better grade) when it includes emotional elements, girls often enjoy the opportunity to share in writing workshops and to engage in poetry, fiction writing, journaling, persuasive writing, songwriting, and more.

Saying all this does not mean girls don't face issues in language arts classes. For many girls, reading and writing do not come easily. The single-sex classroom is a powerful place of focus and vitality for girls' interests in both reading and writing.

One day when the girls were reading poetry— sharing their favorite poems—in Ms. Jaben's classroom, they specifically asked if they could sit around their pretend campfire. After reading her selection, one girl remarked, "This is when I'm really glad to be in single-sex classes."

Providing Reading Choice to Girls

As you set up a reading program for your girls-only classroom, it is often critical to evaluate the books that you and your school ask girls to read. The key question to answer is: Are these choices nurturing girls' reading interests with female role models? Through carefully selected reading that is followed by thoughtful discussion, teachers can help girls overcome stereotypical gender biases, expand their perspectives, and learn more about themselves in the process. Girls constantly report two things: they enjoy many boy-oriented books, but they also want to read more about the roles of women.

> *"It took a few weeks for my girls to become competitive with their grades in language arts because many of them were already achieving and some had never really achieved at all. As soon as the lower performing girls started making better grades in their new single-sex classes, the girls who were already achieving felt they were beginning to lose their 'highest average' standing, so they wanted to improve more. The lower achieving students found out that they could achieve and they continue to study and work hard to prove this to the other girls."*

—Kim Carabo, 8th grade language arts teacher

Teachers need to choose books for girls that provide strong female role models who come from many different cultures and backgrounds, and who struggle to establish their places beyond the traditionally established cultural roles and expectations for women. As girls read books with strong female protagonists, they explore and consider their own natures, define their perspectives, and determine their own direction. Through book discussions, teachers can help girls find their own voices as young women. As one teacher told us, "It's not just about the reading—it's also about the teacher helping girls consider their own character traits, determine what they believe and what they value, and decide how they will act on those beliefs and values."

TRY THIS: Utilize These Resources for Girls' Books

For help in selecting books for girls, check out these resources:

- *Great Books for Girls* by Kathleen Odean
- *100 Books for Girls to Grow On* by Shireen Dodson
- Teenreads.com

- *Once Upon a Heroine: 400 Books for Girls to Love* by Alison Cooper-Mullin & Jennifer Coye

Kathleen Odean said this about how she made her selections for *Great Books for Girls*:

> I looked for girls and women who faced the world without timidity, either from the first or after overcoming their fears. I found female characters who are creative, capable, articulate, and intelligent. They solve problems, face challenges, resolve conflicts, and go on journeys. These girls are not waiting to be rescued; they are doing the rescuing. Nor are they waiting for a male to provide a happy ending: They are fashioning their own stories.

Activities to Promote Reading for Girls

Here is a short list of activities to promote expanded reading among girls. These have been provided by teachers in girls-only classes.

- Have girls make book lists, recommending their favorite books and decorating their list with symbols and pictures that represent the books they have selected. Display these for all students to see. When girls recommend books to each other, there is a stronger chance that they will read these selections.

- Host a "Girls' Book Club Party," outdoor café style, with refreshments. Set up card tables and chairs. Have each girl talk briefly about the book she is reading, while the club enjoys refreshments. Then allow time for silent reading. To make it more fun, let the girls make hats to wear to the party.

- Suggest that girls and their mothers (or aunts, grandmothers, guardians) read the same book and discuss it with other mothers and daughters. This can happen at school or as an evening book club event. The books, of course, should appeal to girls and be age appropriate. You might consider partnering with your local public library to offer a program like this. Libraries have wonderful community outreach programs, and can sometimes even provide modest funding!

- Use the Great Books-Junior Great Books format for teaching important literacy skills for reading comprehension, critical thinking, listening, speaking, and writing. Great Books discussions help students read for meaning and learn to support their interpretations. They involve students in discussions that answer questions of fact, questions of interpretation, questions of value, and questions of evaluation. Teachers can learn about the objectives, skills, and strategies involved in leading Great Books discussions through the Great Books Foundation at www.greatbooks.org.

- Require girls to mark interesting passages for further discussion in class. Have them use sticky notes on chapter pages to record questions that come to mind as they read, or to cite examples of specific traits exhibited by a character (such as integrity, courage, determination).

- Use reading groups in the classroom so that girls can talk about what they read. They will pick up on small but important details they missed; see how others viewed the reading differently; be more open-minded about subjects they have had little experience with in the past; and identify themes of the book which they had not previously considered.

"One thing that has helped me read more critically and thoughtfully this year is having book groups for discussing reading. Discussing reading with others helped me realize more of the important elements. My group members brought up questions and thoughts about the book that made me think differently, and when I had a question, it was easier to get an answer discussing it with the group. Even though I thought I was a pretty good reader (and I am), I was surprised at how much the group helped me develop my critical reading skills."

—Cassie, 8th grade girl

Exploring Writing Opportunities with Girls

Girls are full of lively stories and unique ideas about their world. On any given day, teachers watch girls telling stories about things that have happened to them— at home, at school, in their dreams. Often, though, there are girls who don't write well. They can't bring their storytelling to the printed page.

In girls-only classrooms, girls can be encouraged to write their own personal stories and share them with others in ways that would not be as easy in coed classrooms with boys around. Also, when themes that are essential to girls are the focus of a paper, even girls who have difficulty writing can think more deeply—discovering what they already know, considering what they want to say, practicing creative thought, and feeling the power of putting words on paper.

Especially for those girls who have writing difficulties, try something that might at first seem radical—a rap activity that has been used successfully by a number of teachers. You can have girls create a rap that includes information on a particular curriculum topic. They can write the rap and then perform it for their peers. It can be used to review information about nouns, dinosaurs, sustainability, or any topic. This rap was created by Carolina Day teacher Susan White as a fun way to review correct punctuation skills:

McGrammar

Come on people, don't be dense;
learn to write a proper sentence.
Bring your mind back from vacation
to the basics of punctuation.
Two sentences joined with just a comma
will surely cause your teacher trauma.
This simply won't suffice;
It's called a comma splice.
But if the sentences are related,
You will make me so elated,
if you use a semicolon;
then our grammar will be rollin'.
This little comma can also function
When joining sentences with a conjunction.
A colon stands for "for example,"
and your sentence will be ample
when it follows a complete sentence;
Mess this up and you'll do penance.
It's used for listing or defining.
(The other colon's used for dining.)

Help Girls Keep Journals

Journal writing is a great way for girls to reflect on the experiences that shape their lives, and they often enjoy the opportunity to sit down together and record personal entries. For girls having trouble with writing assignments, a daily journal can be very helpful for writing growth.

As a teacher, not only can you assign journal writing, but you can also open the class to group sharing. If a girl wants to share what she has written, reading aloud can be a powerful classroom activity.

Whether teachers use journal writing as a way for students to polish their skills or to write freely without concern about form, there are many ways that journaling can benefit girls. Research shows that journal writing

- Builds confidence in writing
- Allows girls to express themselves
- Gets the class calm and focused, especially when the writing is a routine that occurs at the beginning of language arts classes
- Helps girls learn to write more fluently
- Allows girls to look back and see how their writing has improved
- Gives girls a chance to vent
- Helps teachers get to know students better (when writing is not confidential)
- Provides an opportunity to share something important with an adult

If you are looking for prompts that are effective for journal writing, these have been found helpful by teachers in girls-only classrooms:

- Explain a quotation
- Describe a dream

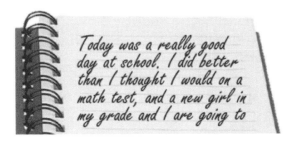

- Tell about a lesson learned

- Write about an event that changed you

- Talk about a mistake you made

- Describe a vacation you would like to take

- Describe a friendship that has been meaningful

- Write a piece of advice for someone you know and care about

- Write a reflection on a reading passage or chapter of a book

Journal writing can provide lighter moments and opportunities for girls to take a break, be themselves, and ponder what is happening. It can also help girls deal with their worries, work out their frustrations, share their disappointments, and even disagree. Here are two such journal entries that middle school girls have chosen to share. Feel free to use them to inspire your own students to write in their journals.

April 3, 2007

Today in class we had a conversation about why people voted for the Nazi's. We also talked about the risks people would take to stand up to the Nazi's and how some even took their side. When my teacher said that, it hit me very hard. I am a Jewish girl and it hurts me to think anyone voted for the Nazi group. I do not understand how one horrible man could get in power and kill six million of my religion. That one man killed people with moms, dads, brothers, and sisters. I just can not comprehend why people would side with such a horrible group.

When we talked about the risk people would have to take to save the Jews, my teacher said that it would have been very hard to save someone back during the Holocaust. In my opinion, even if it means risking your life for something that is right, you should. I did not agree with my teacher today, and I took it very emotionally. I think that everyone should have tried and stopped the war, even if it meant risking their lives. It might have been difficult, but it would have been worth it just to save one more person's life.

The few people who saved the Jews by helping them hide and get away are my heroes. My grandfather was in the Holocaust and had to flee out of Romania. They were a wealthy Jewish family and had many connections. My great grandparents took my grandfather and his siblings to an airport, bribed the pilot with money, and got a flight to Sweden. When they got there, Christian families took them in and helped them get to Canada safely. Those people who helped my family and other families are my heroes, and I hope that if a tragedy like this happened again, I would have that same courage like my heroes.

The war was a horrible event in history. One horrible man started it and many amazing people tried to stop it. The power was too strong and the knowledge was too weak. Today our world is changed from it, just as my family changed from it. 11 million is not just a number, it is many lives. Lives with meaning and history, lives that could have had a future . . . all taken away by one man, one power, and one thought.

—An 8th grade girl

I can't stop thinking about a boy named Paul. He went to my old school and was treated so poorly. My heart aches whenever I try to imagine what he must go through. All of the kids made fun of him right infront of his face! It angered me so much! Just because he was smart and had a different culture. I tried to tell people not to make fun of him, but I wasn't persistent. I never made fun of him, but I just stood by and did nothing. I am ashamed of myself now that I look back on the issue. It deeply saddens me that people have to put others down just to feel more superior.

HELPING GIRLS LEARN SOCIAL STUDIES

When it comes to assessing the performance of boys and girls in schools, math, science, and language arts (reading and writing) garner most of the attention. Although math and science are often discussed regarding girls' achievement issues, and language arts and literacy regarding boys' issues, the progress that girls and boys can make in social studies receives less focus. Our research shows fascinating gains and wonderful tools coming out of single-sex classrooms. Here are some of the innovations.

Mindmapping® has been a big success in Dru Alexander's single-sex classes. It can be a very useful tool for helping girls think abstractly.

Dru told us, "I have been requiring girls and boys to make mindmaps of our units of study and having them include interdisciplinary connections between what they study in language arts, social studies and science." Dru has her students follow the rules in Joyce Wycoff's book, *Mindmapping,* and she gives them plenty of time to reflect on what they are learning. "They all use color, and most of the girls add lots of visual designs. Girls also tend to write a lot of detail that helps them review a topic. Mindmapping is a great way for girls to make sense of what

they have learned, and I often use them as an alternative means of assessing student understanding."

In another project, Dru gave her girls' and boys' classes choices for their Civil War projects. The boys made Civil War baseball cards of famous generals. The girls, on the other hand, made **Abolitionist Freedom Quilt Projects**. Using the traditional patterns of the freedom quilts or "code" quilts, girls recreated colorful representations of the designs on eight-by-eight-inch cards, and on the back of each design they wrote facts about the abolitionists. Whereas the boys enjoyed getting into the gory details of war, the girls were far more interested in learning about the anti-slavery abolitionist movement.

Fifth-grade teacher Mignon Mandon describes another Civil War project that also highlights the different directions girls and boys may take when doing the same task.

> We do a Civil War biography project that involves students becoming class experts on an important person during the Civil War. Students choose an important historical person of the era, type biography information and cut the information into strips, and then make a 3-D model of the person. The model of the person is then attached to a tin can and the can is filled with the bio strips. Students present their information by pulling the strips out of the can as they report. The boys like the aspect of choosing generals and important men and the girls love to study about famous women who made a significant mark in history. The girls also love the artistic aspect of making the model. While everyone makes a model, the boys and girls end up with very different "looks" for their projects.

As you teach girls-only classrooms, remember that an important resource for your school is the **National Coalition of Girls' Schools**. The coalition seeks grants and forms partnerships with businesses to make programs available for teachers. These programs and the information on their Web site (www.ncgs.org) are helpful to teachers who want to learn more about cultivating girls' natural interest in learning.

Indeed, there are many more organizations coming into existence every year that can help you enjoy your girls-only classroom. Perhaps the common theme

in all of them is boosting confidence through girl-friendly learning of key topics, such as core curricula. And not surprisingly, wherever you turn for advice you may notice that girls, like boys, crave relationships, and crave them in their own way. Our final chapter will focus on the unique relationships you can develop in a single-sex classroom.

WRAPPING UP THE MAIN POINTS

Though many girls are doing very well in school, there are still important areas where they need our help. In working with girls in your single-sex classroom, keep these issues in mind:

- Research indicates that girls need to experience more success in math, science, and technology and to understand the career opportunities available to them in related fields.

- To do well in math, science, and technology, girls need success early in school, gaining confidence in their abilities—this confidence can be developed by having lots of hands-on, spatial development opportunities.

- Girls connect through relationships, so it's important for them to be able to see how content that is presented relates to their lives.

- Girls need to be exposed to female role models in nontraditional fields who can help them see what is possible.

- Teachers can help girls learn to use their skills with words in healthy, positive ways and discourage the negative verbal behavior that sometimes becomes problematic.

Many of these issues can be easily addressed in the comfort zones created by a single-sex classroom.

Building Relationships Through Single-Sex Experiences

I go to four coed classes and two single-sex classes per day. At first, I liked the coed classes better, then I liked the single-sex ones better. Now I like some things about each better. One thing I really noticed in my girl-only science class is how much closer I feel to my teacher. It is a great feeling!

—Emma, 9th grade girl

Boys and girls of all ages crave strong connections with caring adults at home and at school. When students have meaningful attachments to adults, they are more likely to care about learning, more likely to be in school, and more likely to stay in school. In all schools this is true; in single-sex classrooms, it is true in boy-friendly and girl-friendly ways. What we mean by this is that the single-sex environment creates rather unique opportunities for relationship building that can directly support good instruction.

Though there is probably never going to be a way to disaggregate "relationships" from other variables, and thus to "prove" that the unique templates of male-male and female-female relationships in single-sex environments enhance learning, anecdotal and testimonial evidence from teachers and students suggests a certain kind of relational "magic" that happens in many single-sex environments, a kind of relational comfort you can maximize in your classroom. Much of what we provide in this chapter can be used in coed classrooms as well.

TRY THIS: Practical Ways to Enhance Relationships Right Now

To help students in your single-sex class bond with one another and with you from the very beginning, try some of these strategies. These are successful techniques provided to us by teachers in single-sex classrooms.

- Share stories to help students connect with you and to each other.

- Teach important values.

- Engage students in interesting ways.

- Reveal your true self. Appropriate self-disclosure makes a teacher more real and more worthy of trust.

- Show students that you have made mistakes too.

- Read aloud to your students. Share your voice, your passion, your enthusiasm, even your funny faces.

- Dress up to teach a concept. Become a superhero—"Amazing Word Man," "Ms. Gravity" or "Mr. Manners"—to make a point or to teach a lesson students won't forget.

- Within the bounds of appropriateness, play music that your students think is cool, and ask the girls or the boys why it is cool to them.

- Hold students to high expectations.

- Manage your classroom with authority. Students want to be in classrooms where the teacher is leading the learning activities and where students know and respect the boundaries.

- Give some freedom of choice and trust—with guidance and support students will amaze you with what they create.

- Use humor to add fun and make things less serious. Laughter actually gets more oxygen to the brain, increasing the level of endorphins in the blood, reducing stress and making us feel better. Think you're not funny? Then find jokes and cartoons to share with your students. They will appreciate your lighthearted approach, and they'll want you to continue it throughout the year.

- Avoid nasty sarcasm, the kind that can undermine any sense of support that you may be trying to give to students.

- Let students know you are open to talking with them about important issues, including how their peer relationships are going.

THE IMPORTANCE OF RELATIONSHIP BUILDING

There has been substantial dialogue in the last decade regarding how important it is for students to become adults who possess "soft skills." The consensus definition of soft skills seems to be "skills that involve the ability to interact and communicate positively and productively with other people." Purdue University's Center for Career Opportunities has created a list of soft skills that includes work ethic, courtesy, teamwork, self-discipline, self-confidence, conformity to prevailing norms, and language proficiency. To be successful in today's and tomorrow's job markets, workers need a combination of occupation-specific technical skills and the applicable soft skills.

A number of teachers in single-sex classrooms, especially those from middle and high schools, have told us that once the male-female pubertal distractions are removed, they can help students focus on their own "soft skills development" more easily. These teachers find they are not adding yet another agenda item to an already full instructional curriculum, but rather that they are integrating topics and skills into everyday group dynamics among males and females.

Here are a number of the soft skills these teachers are integrating. See if you are using, teaching, or integrating these.

• *Communication skills* are needed one-on-one and in groups. Do you model good listening skills and ways to provide positive critical feedback, without being too judgmental? Boys tend to offer impulsive negative comments to peers (often meant as humor), and girls tend to smile while gossiping about peers behind their back. These habits can begin early, and your single-sex classroom is a place where you can better monitor students and guide them toward appropriate communication skills. Usually you have to use correction, modeling, and group discussion to succeed in this area.

• *Written communication skills* are important both in written work and online communications. We touched on concerns about communication in cyberspace in an earlier chapter, and learning good cyberetiquette is crucial for all children, as they will often be functioning in a work world that includes a virtual arena. Many parents are not teaching these skills, but your classroom can become a place for safe discussion, especially about consequences for cybergossip and cyberviolence.

• *Teamwork and collaboration skills* help students work productively with others to accomplish a group goal. This skill is more and more important in all areas of work, and needs to be taught through practice. Both boys and girls learn important lessons about the dynamics of working with teams in single-sex classrooms, and this seems to translate well into coed environments, especially when augmented with good listening skills!

• *Risk-taking skills* come more naturally to boys but can be encouraged for girls (and shy boys) in single-sex settings. This skill helps students to be more willing to try something new, different, or unknown rather than never straying from their comfort zone. Research shows boys will venture more fully into literature and the arts in single-sex classes, whereas girls will take on the challenges of math, science, and technology more assertively. The single-sex environment itself, therefore, appears to encourage risk taking; you can build on this by showing students when they are avoiding risk, and asking them why.

CONNECTING WITH GIRLS

Karen Boyk has been teaching a model single-sex all-girls class in a coed public middle school in Michigan for over twelve years. The class meets for two class periods each day, covering the two subjects for which Karen is "highly-qualified"—introduction to algebra and language arts. She "blocks" the courses, so that on Monday and Wednesday the girls have language arts for two class periods, on Tuesday and Thursday they have math for two class periods, and on Friday they do both, or just one, depending on what's going on. This helps with the students' workload, because they often have two nights to complete assignments.

Karen's class is optional; parents sign their daughters up for the class. For the past twelve years it has been a popular choice for girls and each year there is a lottery for participation in the class. According to their feedback to Karen, "The girls and I love it!!"

One way Karen uses this single-sex model to really connect with the girls is through the use of class meetings.

She says,

> Middle school girls create drama, and much of it is often caused by gossip, stories being told and retold, girls sharing things with others that they promised not to tell, etc. In my class, we have a class meeting about once every two weeks or so. We arrange the desks in a circle, so we can all see each other. I usually give them a couple of topics to discuss—opinion on something happening in the school, report cards, and the like, but I also tell them they can talk about anything they want. We go around the circle, and in the first round, every girl must speak and no one interrupts. Then we go around one or two more times, and they can pass or add to the discussion.
>
> In the beginning of the year, the girls are rather skeptical to share much, but as the year goes on, the trust builds and some of the things the girls have to say are amazing. Often in class meetings, girls are able to share with the entire class at one time something they'd like to tell—family issues like divorce, when their dog dies, family illnesses. It's so much easier to "get it out all at once" and not have to keep retelling a story. I've had girls laugh and cry as they share the happy and tragic events in their lives.

I've been asked about using class time for something that's not part of the curriculum. Yes, class meetings do cut into my instructional time; however, I have found it is time well spent. Just because you are teaching a lesson doesn't mean their mind isn't elsewhere! By using meetings to discuss what is important to the girls in a structured forum, I find that they spend less time when we are working on academic material gossiping and whispering.

Teachers like Karen who want to connect with girls often begin by demonstrating how much they care about the girls. Girls notice when a teacher cares because it is obvious in the teacher's voice and in the teacher's eyes. Girls see caring teachers as those who honestly and sincerely want to know them as individuals and who practice patience, show trust, warmth, and encouragement. They see teachers who care about girls as the ones who want them to be happy and successful inside the classroom but who also care about their lives outside of school.

"I like Mrs. Gallager because she always asks us what we did over the weekend, how we are feeling and will always give us information on herself and how she is doing."

—Lena, 8th grade girl

Practically speaking, teachers who care for girls

- Listen to what they say, paying attention and understanding their messages
- Nurture them with kind, gentle, and encouraging words, without babying them
- Are friendly and supportive, while maintaining appropriate teacher roles
- Promote enthusiasm for the subjects they teach
- Understand the concerns of girls and value their questions
- Teach girls to do things without doing things for them

- Hold girls in mutual respect, and respect confidentiality when appropriate

- Are available to girls to discuss their concerns, answer their questions, share their excitement, and so on

- Demonstrate a sense of fun and a willingness to participate in learning with them

- Sense when girls are having problems (by noticing drops in academic or athletic performance, loss of interest in things that mattered before, self-cutting, talk of suicide, sudden changes in friendships, isolation, anger, unusual weight gain or loss, lack of sleep, decrease in communication, uncommon attention-seeking behavior, suspected drug or alcohol use), and find ways to assist them

- Help girls prepare for the future—what is coming tomorrow, what is coming next week, what is coming next year—making transitions easier

Providing Discipline to Girls

Although classroom discipline is an issue that relates more frequently to boys than girls (in the United States, on average, 90 percent of discipline referrals to the principal are for boys), the way teachers manage their girls-only classroom is important. Here is a short list of suggestions that make a real difference in this regard.

Teachers who successfully manage girls-only classrooms

- Clearly identify expectations and consequences for girls.

- Use mistakes and failures as teaching tools by discussing the process of emotions that led to the mistake.

- Talk specifically about the problem and the desired behavior and do not accept excuses the second time around.

- Carefully avoid embarrassing the girl—if the girl gets severely embarrassed, she will tend to harbor resentment and seek revenge, making future behavior more undisciplined.

- Are willing to spend more time talking with girls about their issues and their feelings than boys might need. This is especially important for male teachers to realize.

- Encourage girls, before problems arise, to work at becoming less sensitive to constructive criticism and directness.

In applying all these techniques, teachers notice that if they can bond with girls at the outset of the class, they can more easily manage discipline as situations arise. The bonding also helps girls more readily trust the teacher's discipline. The end result is that girls will come to like their teacher and want to do what is right for her or him.

"Speed Talking"—Connecting Girls with Older Girls for Mentoring

A primary area in girls' relationships in which you may have to engage is "the drama." The drama that can exist among middle school girls is natural but, at the same time, can be quite destructive to their social culture. This is often the case with seventh-grade girls who are typically overly focused on social status and peer relationships at a time when their lives are also becoming more complicated by their growing interest in boys.

Barb King and Bebe Zazzaro are school counselors at Carolina Day who deal with girl issues on a daily basis. To address some of the social concerns that their seventh-grade girls were facing, they decided to try a new approach. Believing that the seventh-grade girls would benefit from the opportunity to learn from some older girls—and feeling that the younger girls might be more open to hearing any wisdom and insights from older girls, rather than from adult teachers or counselors—they invited girls from the high school to lead an activity they named **Speed Talking**. Together, the counselors and high school girls designed this two-hour activity to focus on helping seventh-grade girls become more **comfortable**, **connected**, and **confident** as middle school students.

In this activity, the counselors meet with the high school volunteers beforehand and ask them to be ready to share things they remember about their own middle school experience, and to describe lessons they feel they learned. Then the speed talking session itself begins with a pizza lunch (it can be an after-school activity as well). Preselected groups of five seventh-grade girls are seated at tables to share pizza with two high school girls. These initial conversations exist simply to provide an opportunity for the girls to get to know each other. Once the girls eat, the "speed talking" activity begins, using a format similar to the popular adult activity, "speed dating."

Two high school girls sit at each table with five seventh-grade girls. After approximately ten minutes, the high school girls move to the next table of girls. The speed talking comes to an end once each pair of high school girl rotates through each seventh-grade table. This is only the first half of the speed talking activity, but already, wonderful things happen for the girls. In one case, one of the older girls shared with the younger girls that it had taken awhile, but she had finally stopped worrying about being popular. She discovered that when she surrounded herself with real friends who made her feel comfortable, she was happier and more comfortable herself.

Another of the older girls said that she had very different interests from her best friend in middle school. She always worried that if she did what she liked, instead of what her friend liked, she would risk losing the friendship. Finally, when she took the risk—choosing to spend more time pursuing her own interests, instead of those of her best friend—she was surprised to discover that it did not change their relationship. She was pleased that she was able to keep her friend and, at the same time, make more friends who shared her interests. She said that she had also learned that if the friendship had changed, that would have been okay too. The younger girls, whose issues with friends often haunted them, were deeply moved by hearing that the older girls had gone through similar dramas—and persevered.

The second phase of this activity involves the seventh-grade girls doing the talking. They rotate and ask questions of the older girls. Their questions have ranged from how to get along with parents, how to get parents to trust you, how to get boys to notice you, how to keep friends, to how to balance school and sports.

In the wrap-up phase of the activity, each girl is invited to share an aspect of the event that resonated with her. In some cases girls have simply chosen to express gratitude for the event. Others have expressed the knowledge they gained. Others have said the activity helped boost their confidence. Others have expressed thanks for access to new high school acquaintances and role models.

This speed talking activity can be replicated in any class, and provides deep learning for girls in soft skills of communication and "hard skills" of character.

Girls Want to Belong—Building Character and Responsibility Through Activities

Girls gain confidence and feel more positive and connected when they participate with other girls on a team. They want to connect with teachers. They enjoy female role models and mentors. And they can come to rely deeply on coaches. In all of these relationships, they are naturally forming girl teams by which to survive and thrive.

Like boys, girls need coaches, mentors, and team leaders who hold them to high expectations. When girls sign up to be a part of a team, their coach or advisor will quickly set the tone for the experience. Sometimes, coaches miss the fact that girls want to be held to high standards in all that they do, not just in the classroom. Teachers in girls-only classrooms have told us, "I've seen more clearly now how girls benefit from an experience that pushes them to go beyond what they thought they could do" and that "girls want to be pushed, all while working together as a unit and being held to high expectations." The coach or sponsor who enjoys working with girls and believes that they should be held to appropriate high standards of performance—whether in dance, drama, basketball, a competitive school club, or another activity—will be valued and admired by girls. That is a good feeling indeed.

"As a girls' basketball coach, it bothers me when people hold boys and girls to different standards in competitive sports. When a boys' team loses, adults often send the message to boys that they need to be 'warriors' and work harder. But, with girls, it is often the case that they are much less concerned with a loss, frequently brushing it off by telling girls that they look and act nice as a team. That's a very different message."

—John Zazzaro, high school teacher and coach

TRY THIS: Team Activities for Girls

Not all girls will like all these activities, but they can try more than one, and enjoy doing them with other girls.

- Sports, sports, sports! Girls love to participate and compete. There are so many lessons for girls to learn through sports—about motivation and self-confidence, how to win and lose, how to compete, and how to work with others. Sports help girls learn how to assess their skills and surpass their perceived limitations. Consider coaching a school team. It is a great way to connect with girls!

- Consider bringing girls and boys together for a few ballroom dance lessons during the school day. To inspire them, first let students watch the 2005 documentary "Mad Hot Ballroom." Be sure to choose the instructor carefully—one who will appeal and relate to the age group. Offer the instruction during PE class for several weeks. Be sure to give students enough lessons to make them feel competent in dancing at least two ballroom dances. Then consider asking the DJ at the next school dance to play a few tunes that will allow students to show off their skills. You may just start something special for your school!

- Start a Girl Scout troop at your school. Girl Scouts includes an international counterpart, Girl Guides. This organization works with girls around the world in a character-building, nurturing program that helps girls gain skills and experiences in leadership, social conscience, and self-worth for success in a real world. You can find more information at www.girlscouts.org.

- Start an after-school girls' service club. Consider activities that will help girls feel a part of solving problems in their community and the world. Ideas include

  - raking leaves for the elderly or handicapped

  - adopting a military team—sending postcards, thank-you notes, notes of encouragement, care packages, cookies

  - planting bulbs at a local park or adult care facility

  - adopting a homeless shelter—providing meals, playing with the children who live there, donating and reading children's books, hosting a blanket, coat, and toy drive

> - having an environmental clean-up day—invite parents and the greater community
> - Take girls as a group on a hiking or camping trip—consider a star-gazing trip where girls learn about constellations

CONNECTING WITH BOYS

"My boys greet me each day as they enter the classroom. They have the choice of a hug, a high five, a handshake, an octopus shake (open fingers wide and wrap them around her fingers. I always say something to each boy like, 'I am glad you are here today, Zach.' At the mid-point in the year, all the boys have chosen to give me a hug each morning. I tell my boys, 'We are family and we treat each other that way.' We have a song we sing called 'This is our school family,' and we have another song we sing on the day when any boy is absent, 'We wish you well.'"

—Tessa Michaelos, kindergarten teacher

Boys crave strong connections with adults and long for a sense of "belonging" at school. They want to be understood, listened to, taken seriously, and respected by adults and by their peers. Especially for boys who are "at risk" in today's schools, reconnecting to learning via connections with others can enhance success.

Practically speaking, teachers who care for boys often show that care by

- Holding boys to standards of respect for others
- Offering frequent opportunities for participation and practice of skills
- Showing boys practical strategies for success, and promulgating fair and clear expectations of success
- Applying consistent rules for behavior and fair discipline to help boys manage their lives and relationships
- Helping boys avoid or respond to ridicule, so that they do not lose respect in front of their peers

- Serving as male role models to look up to and emulate, both in behavior and in teaching of wisdom

- Showing boys what they can achieve by working hard, and why the goals asked of them are relevant to their lives as young men

- Recognizing when boys may be in pain (by noticing increased absences from school, diminished self-esteem, not talking, difficulty getting along with peers, fighting, lying, cheating, speaking about or treating girls with disrespect, poor grades, not doing homework, failing to take responsibility, sitting alone, avoiding activities or games where sides are chosen), and finding both private and official ways to help them

- Helping boys learn ways to express their feelings and address their emotional needs as young men

Middle school teacher Bebe Zazzaro is a strong believer in talking to boys about how their brains work and what their bodies need to be healthy. She tells them why they feel differently about things than girls do and why they behave differently too. The boys she teaches in the single-sex classroom find great comfort in her understanding, and often show up at her door to ask questions.

On one occasion, a boy stopped in to ask, "Ms. Z, you know so much about boys. My legs hurt all the time, and I want to know why. Can you tell me?" Of course, she asked if he had shared this with his parents and his doctor, but then she reminded him of how quickly he was growing, telling him how important

it was to stretch his limbs, get plenty of sleep, include calcium in his diet, and drink lots of water. Boys do want to know things, and they will ask when they feel someone cares and truly knows them.

Teachers can't substitute for other professionals. At the same time, many teachers of boys in single-sex classrooms have noticed that if they develop rapport with their boys as a group through activities and attitudes such as those we just listed, then the individual boys seem more likely to confide in the teacher. The supposition among professionals studying this dynamic is that when boys feel cared for in groups, they feel safer as individuals.

"When looking for teachers to lead our single-gender classrooms, I wanted the teacher who relates to students and develops relationships that go far beyond state curriculum standards. I wanted the teacher who understands that students do not care how much you know, until they know you care about them. The teacher must have the capabilities of establishing camaraderie between themselves and the students they teach."

—Al Darby, high school principal, Georgia

The Special Role of Male Teachers

A challenge that many of the boys you work with may face is the scarcity of fathers, grandfathers, male mentors, and male teachers—often only a few or sometimes no positive, influential men in their lives. Boys who have no strong male role models have far less chance to succeed in life—a primary reason is that they do not get an inchoate sense while growing up of how a male finds his purpose and meaning in a lifetime. These boys grow up with a huge hole inside them, one they often fill later on with drugs, alcohol, withdrawal from society, and violence.

As the number of fatherless boys increases in our culture, the work of creating boys-only environments can become even more important. And even in homes where fathers are present, well-intentioned adult males may not have the vocabulary, skills, or a level of comfort to communicate and guide boys through their social, academic, and emotional problems. Boys today often live with a vast hunger for attention from healthy adult males. Each individual boy needs adult males in his life to whom he can turn for help and advice. Sometimes, that person can be a male teacher.

Among single-sex schools, there is also a thread of male-male experience between teachers and students that is often missed in educational studies—the role of the male who is not an athlete, but instead an artist. Boys in boys-only environments are often very receptive to men who give them opportunities to view the arts from a male perspective. Boys benefit greatly from watching men act, draw, paint, sing, dance, and create. These experiences increase the likelihood that boys will discover hidden interests for the arts, making boys less likely to view the arts as "more for girls."

As you work in your single-sex environment, consider hiring charismatic male teachers to meet the needs of boys. These teachers will build special relationships with some boys, and may quite literally save these boys' lives. Even many female teachers, such as Mrs. Z., who work wonderfully with boys, have shared with us the importance of male teachers. These teachers can see the hunger in boys' eyes for connection to a male mentor.

TRY THIS: Hire Male Teachers Who Understand Boys

If you are involved right now in hiring teachers for boys-only classes, consider hiring male teachers who

- Are able and willing to share their feelings

- Have struggled with adversity and succeeded

- Believe in boys, even when they make mistakes

- Do not prejudge boys, but listen to them and try to guide them appropriately

- Encourage boys to be active participants in one or more areas that can lead to success and recognition—even if that activity is not typically viewed as a masculine activity

- Talk with boys about the things they see, hear, and experience every day—on the Internet, on TV, in music, in video games—making sure boys are savvy about processing and evaluating the information they receive through the media

- Willingly discuss bullying, ridicule, teasing, put downs in order to help boys develop and practice empathy for others

---

One of the places where we do see a lot of males already working in boys-only environments is in athletics and sports. From a number of single-sex schools, we have garnered this short list of the qualities possessed by the kind of coach that works best for boys (and girls):

- Provides a quality experience for each athlete—with an emphasis on instruction, participation, and growth.
- Contributes to each player's mental, emotional, and physical well-being.
- Responds to the developmental needs of the athletes. These coaches delight in the successes of their team, but also help their players learn from their disappointments.
- Helps student athletes gain a greater knowledge of their own physical and athletic potential.
- Builds self-respect in students as they learn to set goals and accomplish them.
- Fosters a deeper understanding of the responsibilities of being a team member.
- Develops practices of good sportsmanship and fair play.
- In the younger grades, requires that cooperation take precedence over competition.
- In the middle grades, begins the process of building competitive teams by concentrating on developing skills and improving each student's overall athletic ability. (Participation should be a key component of the middle school athletic experience, with emphasis more on improving performance than on competition.)
- In the high school grades, encourages teams and players to test their skills in competition at the highest level.
- Educates parents about the school's athletic philosophy and defines the role of parents in supporting that philosophy.

Helping Boys with Their Emotional Lives

_____

"The first year [of single-sex classes] we gave students an emotional IQ test called the Peirs-Harris Emotional Test. We administered it in the

beginning of the year and again at the end. Our hopes were that the students' self esteem would rise and they would feel better about themselves. That is exactly what happened. Both the single-sex classrooms showed improved self-esteem."

—Dave Curtis, 5th grade teacher

A single-sex class can be a powerful place to help boys feel more and discuss their feelings. Sometimes, before parents or teachers put a boy in a boys-only class they may think, "This male environment will stifle feelings." Usually, the opposite is the case. Without girls around, boys often feel more comfortable to express the wide array of their own feelings.

One principal tells a story of a sixth-grade boy who had been in his office on several occasions for being too physical with other boys during recess. Steve participated in games with other boys in his class, but the minute that he felt challenged by another boy's words or actions, he would get angry, hit, kick, or call the boy a name. The principal had several conversations with Steve, followed at times by consequences for his aggressive behavior. But the behavior continued.

One day while trying to give Steve strategies for dealing with his aggressive reactions, the principal encouraged Steve to put the recess games in perspective. After all, what was more important—winning a recess game or having friends? When the principal reminded Steve that it really was "only a game," Steve looked at the principal and told him he was wrong. "It's more than a game," he said. "It's my life." The principal understood suddenly what Steve intuited. The game was, for him, how he found his place in the group.

Boys like Steve want desperately to be accepted and to establish their place in a group, but often feel powerless to do much about it. Steve's social skills were not suited for helping him move up the ladder. His aggressive responses were the only way he knew to jockey for position, so he reacted with anger and aggression toward the very boys he was trying to impress.

For weeks Steve turned his emotions inward and was unable to articulate why he was reacting so aggressively at recess. Finally, Steve's teacher asked all the boys to come together and talk about what was going on. It took a few tries, but Steve and some of the other boys opened up. The teacher clearly saw how boys (mainly in nonverbal ways) encouraged Steve to talk. The teacher also reported that with girls around, there was no way Steve would have shown "weakness" by opening up.

"Unlike girls, boys either harbor problems alone or they are very 'out front' about them—a quick blow up . . . followed by quick intervention . . . and quickly they are back on track. When boys harbor social-emotional problems alone, they need help to realize these are a big deal. Often they say, 'It's all OK. Everything is fine,' when it clearly is not."

—Mignon Mandon

The following list of feelings words is a useful place to start your boys-only class on the journey of coming together to talk about feelings (see chart). You can choose words that work for the grade level and students you teach. It is very helpful to ask boys to recall an incident when they felt one or more of the feelings in this chart. Hearing boys' stories helps other boys feel more.

Activities for Developing a Feeling Vocabulary in Younger Boys

If you are teaching younger boys who don't know these words yet, you can start them on developing a feeling vocabulary in other ways. A good resource for teachers is *Enhancing Emotional Vocabulary in Young Children* by Gail E. Joseph and Phillip S. Strain. They suggest activities such as:

- Have students draw pictures that illustrate how people feel, then discuss the feelings with students. For example, students can draw a picture of a family trip that shows how each of the family members enjoyed the trip. As they draw, remind them to think about how each person was feeling. Talk in private with

A Feeling Vocabulary

Happy	Angry	Valued	Inadequate	Surprised	Afraid	Hurt	Sad
alive	aggravated	accepted	accused	alert	alarmed	abandoned	alone
blissful	agitated	admired	adrift	amazed	anxious	abused	anguished
calm	annoyed	adored	alienated	astounded	apprehensive	blamed	ashamed
carefree	appalled	appreciated	ashamed	awestruck	astonished	censored	blue
cheerful	betrayed	capable	awkward	bewildered	cautious	cheated	bored
delighted	bitter	cherished	beaten down	dazed	cornered	damaged	bummed
ecstatic	burning	competent	belittled	disbelieving	desperate	dashed	burdened
elated	cranky	complete	berated	disillusioned	fearful	deceived	depressed
encouraged	cross	confident	broken	dismayed	frantic	defeated	despondent
energized	disgusted	crazy about	condemned	ecstatic	frightened	deflated	detached
excited	enraged	devoted to	confused	flabbergasted	horrified	demoralized	disillusioned
fabulous	frustrated	fond of	crushed	flustered	humiliated	devastated	disappointed
giddy	fuming	idolized	discarded	immobilized	hurt	diminished	disheartened
glad	furious	loved	excluded	jolted	hysterical	disappointed	downcast
glorious	grouchy	noticed	helpless	mystified	intimidated	heartbroken	gloomy
jolly	grumpy	powerful	hesitant	overwhelmed	jumpy	ignored	guilty
joyful	hostile	proud	ignored	puzzled	leery	intimidated	lonely

(Continued)

A Feeling Vocabulary (*Continued*)

Happy	Angry	Valued	Inadequate	Surprised	Afraid	Hurt	Sad
jubilant	incensed	recognized	incapable	rattled	panicky	jilted	lost
merry	irate	respected	incompetent	sabotaged	paralyzed	put down	low
overjoyed	mad	self-assured	inept	shaken	petrified	shamed	miserable
thrilled	offended	special	inferior	shocked	scared	slighted	morose
tickled	outraged	trusted	judged	startled	shaken	snubbed	sorry
warm	perturbed	whole	mediocre	stunned	tense	upset	sullen
	resentful	worshipped	powerless	traumatized	troubled	wounded	tearful
	seething		rejected		uneasy	wronged	
	steamed		unaccepted		wary		
	ticked off		unworthy		worried		
	troubled		useless				
	upset						

each student, asking him or her to describe the picture and to explain how each person feels. Be sure to write all of the feeling vocabulary on the picture.

- Have book discussions about characters and how they feel. There are many children's books that work well in this regard. As you read, look for situations in which the character is reacting to something emotional, and ask students questions about how the character felt at that moment. Also ask students how they felt when they read that part of the story. With boys, it is often helpful to phrase a question "How do you think the character was feeling?" as it allows the boy a little distance from the actual feelings.

- Have students select words that are synonyms for a particular emotion and rank the words from mild to intense. Here is an example:

Mild			Intense
Happy	Delighted	Thrilled	Ecstatic!

If your boys are very young, they will not know some of these words, but they do know "happy," "sad," and "angry."

- Provide students with a picture book or story containing feeling words (milder versions) from the above emotional vocabulary list, using words appropriate for younger ages, then ask them to replace the milder words with more intense synonyms and see how it changes the story.

"The boys were much more emotionally engaged this year when school counselor Barb King and I decided to have single-sex discussions with middle school students about bullying. In previous coed settings for this purpose, the boys let the girls do most of the talking, and they did not seem to take the discussion seriously. This year, they demonstrated much more awareness of the emotional aspects of bullying, and now I am wondering if we have short-changed boys in the past by addressing this topic in mixed-gender groups. The ways that boys and girls bully and experience bullying can, after all, be quite different, and so is their facility for expressing their feelings in this regard."

—Blake Smith, school counselor

Managing Boy Behavior and Providing Meaningful Discipline

"My grandfather and I talk about how boys get upset and their emotions get the best of them. Then boys act on their emotions before they really think about it. We call that E-A-T (Emotions-Action-Thinking). When I get emotional about something, what I need to do is E-T-A. Emotions, then Thinking, then Action."

—Jonah, 7th grade boy

One of the things we hear clearly from both coed and single-sex schools is the importance of maintaining discipline "through the bonds" not "against the bonds." What this means is that boys will often follow the discipline of a person to whom they are bonded, and more often will not follow the discipline of someone who does not seem to understand them, and is thus not bonded with them.

Another comment we hear constantly is the need to understand how the male brain processes emotion, and thus how males process the discipline they receive. Boys often need very clear explanations for the rules governing their behavior. They need consequences and enforcement. They need teachers to view most boy "errors" as opportunities for teaching, rather than simply as problems. They need consistency and fairness. They desperately need respect. Much of male adolescence is occupied by a hormonal, neurological, and social system in which males are trying to develop their lifelong basis for self-respect.

In schools we work with, we have noticed that some people feel that the best way to get a boy to respond is to dress him down, especially in front of others. This approach can work but often does not. Many boys, following that shaming experience, may well spend lots of time being angry and trying to figure out how to get even. Sometimes adults back boys into corners by calling them down in ways that tear them apart in front of their friends or classmates. If an adult really thinks that the boy will change his personality, open up in front of his friends, and respond to the humiliation with an apology such as, "Oh, you are so right. I'm sorry," that adult is probably quite mistaken.

"In recent years, my increased understanding of how boys react in emotional situations has made such a positive difference in how I discipline them as an elementary principal. In the past when a boy was brought to my office for breaking the rules (most often for hitting or getting in a fight), I used to insist on eye contact. I would lean forward and say firmly, 'Look me in the eye. We are not going to continue until you look at me.' Most often the child would glance up quickly, and then his eyes would immediately dart back down again. I struggled to get information out of boys, and my frustration would increase as a result.

When I read Boys and Girls Learn Differently, *I immediately changed my approach with boys. I no longer expect them to look at me during these tense moments, and I don't rush or pressure them to talk. I ask guiding questions about what happened, but I almost always find that they can't talk about it right away. My most reliable tactic is to give them space by leaving them in the sitting area of my office and returning to my desk (a few feet away) to work. When no words are coming from a boy I will say, 'I'm going to do some work at my desk, and when you are ready to talk, let me know.' Then I move to my desk and start tapping away on my computer. When I give that physical and emotional space, it never takes long for the child to tell me that he is ready to talk—or he just starts talking! At that point, I return to my chair right next to him, and we are able to discuss the situation and resolve it.*

I have also slowed down my pace in my discussions with boys, and I am no longer afraid of silence. I will simply wait, without saying anything, if a boy gets stalled in the midst of telling me his story. This gives him the time to process what has happened and what he is feeling, and to find the words to describe it."

—Claudia Sherry, Carolina Day School

> **TRY THIS: Discipline Techniques for Helping Boys**
>
> You may have already tried many of these techniques, but some might feel new.
>
> - When a boy is upset or in trouble, go for a walk and talk.
> - Don't ask a boy who is in trouble to look you in the eye.
> - When the situation warrants, be the "alpha."
> - Keep messages to boys as short as possible—set a goal of ten words or less.
> - Don't require boys to confess or to discuss feelings during tense moments.
> - Don't make boys sit during recess as punishment—instead have them do physical chores.

SOCIAL STRUCTURES AND ACTIVITIES THAT HELP BOTH BOYS AND GIRLS

We will end this chapter highlighting three areas of social activity that work for boys and girls. These activities—advisory programs, outreach to parents, and community-wide field trips—are general, but can be tailored to gender.

Establishing an Advisory Program

One of the most direct methods available for building relationships and connecting with students is a strong advisory program, especially for middle and high school students. Advisory programs provide a caring adult mentor for each student, with the primary goal of helping young people develop character skills, discover their strengths and passions, and achieve greater success in school and in life. Advisory programs may be difficult to achieve in some schools where the student-to-adult ratio is prohibitive, but when possible, this program can be a valuable asset to building relationships that matter, encouraging student leadership and facilitating effective role modeling for students. Advisors can have a lot of influence on the students they mentor, and when that influence is consistently positive and productive it can change the lives of their advisees in ways that really matter. Peggy Daniels helped develop a model advisory program, which you can replicate and adapt for your school.

In the spring of 2004, about the time that Carolina Day decided to begin single-sex instruction in its sixth and seventh grades, the middle school teachers proposed trying single-sex advisory groups, mixing students from all three grades (6–8). They also wanted to try keeping their advisees together for three years (looping), instead of changing to a new group each year (with eighth graders rotating off each year and new sixth graders being added). They created girls' advisory groups with female advisors or teachers and boys' advisory groups with male advisors (including coaches and staff). They also established a daily advisory period (twenty minutes per day) that meets first thing in the morning, so advisors can assess how each student is doing immediately upon his or her arrival at school.

The teachers cited the following reasons to Peggy for establishing this type of advisory grouping. They felt that it would

- Create strong mentoring relationships among the students and between students and the advisor—emphasizing the bonding and attachment that are so important for success and happiness at this age. Middle school children typically undergo drops in self-esteem during their preadolescent years and the faculty felt the groups were a way to help combat that, especially with same-sex mentors.

- Enhance trust and a sense of belonging among the girls and boys. The seventh- and eighth-grade advisory members wanted the opportunity to provide leadership within their advisory groups, and serve as mentors to younger sixth-grade students.

- Facilitate a feeling of deeper understanding and connection between adults and students across the grades, creating a stronger community. Teachers felt this program would allow and require them to follow more closely what was happening in all three grades.

- Allow advisees to share information about what goes on in their particular grade, enabling students to better understand what happens in other grade levels. Sixth and seventh graders, for example, would hear some of the challenges of being an eighth-grade student and see how eighth graders work through those challenges. Advisors felt this would give students something to look forward to, while helping reduce the stress of moving to the next grade.

- Provide ample opportunities to discuss topics that are important for this age—focusing on the students' immediate social, emotional, and academic needs.

For example, one topic of interest regards how our culture and the media try to create gender uniformity.

- Enable adults and students to safely and privately (within same-sex groupings) address the unique and sex-specific social and emotional stresses that boys and girls deal with at this age.

Peggy and her school are glad to note that the initial vision of the teachers has paid off. The program has led to increased bonding, emotional assistance for boys and girls, real issues being dealt with right away, and enhanced school discipline and camaraderie.

Here are recent comments from two of the adult advisors:

> In my single-sex boy advisory group, there is a lot of camaraderie. Having the older (eighth grade) boys serve as leaders, explaining the schedules, school rules and expectations to the younger (sixth and seventh grade) boys works well. I notice that the boys often prefer activities over discussions, although we often have advisory group discussions three or four times a week. Gym time is valuable for bonding and waking up and energizing in the morning as well as learning how to play fairly together. Boys also do well with games like Pictionary, charades, or Claytionary, involving teamwork and creative and critical thinking. We had a lot of fun making videos on the character theme of compassion. It was a great process as the boys worked together, taking turns as director, cameramen and actors. It would have been much more difficult to engage boys in this type of activity in a coed advisory.
>
> —Jeff Peisner, middle school teacher and advisor

> Earlier this year, the girls in my mixed-grade, single-sex advisory were a little reluctant to talk about their feelings, which surprised me. The dynamics of this particular group seemed different than the other female advisories, and a few of the more dominant girls in my group were somewhat private about discussing such things outside their group of intimates, which is fine. Lately, though, as they get used

to the group, they have been more open and are bonding in other ways—willing to get to know one another and support one another on less private matters. I decided they might benefit from regular opportunities to share in a discussion circle and that has helped them to open up. I have encouraged girls to be more honest and real with each other whenever they can, and I am seeing them take more risks with this. This has become a uniquely important experience for these girls.

—Sandy Pyeatt, middle school teacher and advisor

Establishing Rapport and Building Bonds with Parents

Parent education and parent involvement have an enormous impact on students' attitudes and performance in any school. Some parents don't want to be involved with their children's schools or schoolwork; others want very much to be involved. Especially in single-sex programs, outreach to parents is essential, not just because the program may at first feel novel and even uncomfortable to parents, but also because moms and dads (and other extended family members) can find immediate connections to their girl or boy via volunteer work in a single-sex class.

Here are some suggestions, already proven successful in single-sex programs, for developing and strengthening school-parent partnerships:

- Invite parents to parent evening lectures in which you teach them about the learning differences between girls and boys. Share books with parents about developmental stages and brain development in boys and girls.

- In parent conferences and parent evenings, openly discuss boy energy and how you deal with it at school. Explain the importance of recess, breaks, PE, sports, and intramural programs.

- Ask parents to come in and help with special PE-type activities. Perhaps there are parents who could teach a few lessons in some area (such as basketball skills, ballroom dancing, or gymnastics).

- Teach parents that developing empathy in boys is an important goal—and one of our best hopes for leading boys away from violence and toward an understanding of what it means to be a responsible, caring man.

- Make parents of girls aware of their enormous influence on their daughters' self-perceptions of their bodies and minds. In parent evenings and through books and handouts, help parents navigate their girls' rises and falls in adolescent self-esteem. Parents find this to be a huge gift, and often bond with teachers and programs that help them in this way.

- Share information with parents about how the media influences our boys and girls (TV, ads, magazines, Internet, video games). Newsletters, parent evenings, and parent conferences can be good outlets for this information. Share research not just about how a particular medium—video games or the Internet—affects boys or girls, but also about how hours in front of a screen affects the brains of young children.

- Share information about stress and its effects on learning, including the potential challenges faced by an overscheduled child. Parents often don't realize that their boy or girl does not have to do five activities a day to be a success.

- Work with parents to create homework policies that clarify the different roles of parents, students, and teachers. Place value on time at home to relax and be with family.

- Educate and constantly remind parents about the importance of good nutrition, adequate sleep, and hydration. Many parents are not aware of what is good for a boy or girl. Your advice is not a physician's advice, but you can certainly "turn parents on" to resources they have not known about before. Most parents are deeply grateful.

- Enlist the help of parents in supporting all children through character education—helping kids be less judgmental, more accepting of differences, less concerned about social positioning, less tolerant of relational aggression or bullying, and more confident, strong, and courageous in terms of standing up for what is right.

- When helpful, establish contracts with parents: "This is what we do. This is what you do."

- Seek information from parents about the interests and characteristics of their boys and their girls. "What are Johnny's strengths?" "Where does Julie excel?"

- Encourage fathers to attend PTA or PTO meetings just as they would attend sporting events.

Activities That Meld Together the Community of Parents, Teachers, and Students

As we end this chapter, we are including activities that single-sex programs have utilized with success to build bonds between the school, the students, and the parents as a holistic community. These activities and others like them can help you direct the triangle of student-teacher, parent-student, and parent-teacher bonds into a circular, interconnected, and united community.

- Ask parents to volunteer to help your class with a local service project (usually by driving, at least).

- Go with boys or girls and families to a local camp to participate in a ropes course or climbing wall activity. Do this with a particular grade each year and see it as an important rite-of-passage event—something for students to look forward to as they enter a particular grade. They will have the opportunity to cooperate and encourage their classmates—developing stronger bonds—and they will experience a sense of accomplishment from the challenge. Doing this in single-sex groupings can be especially helpful for girls, who are often intimidated by boys who like to show off their physical prowess during such activities.

- Have a tie-tying relay event. Everyone (boys and girls) needs to learn how to tie a necktie or put a tie knot in a scarf. Ask parents to send in some old neckties and scarves and practice in your advisory for a couple of weeks, making sure that everyone can successfully tie a tie. (If you don't collect enough ties and scarves, ask your local secondhand store for a donation!) Then have

a school tie-tying relay race where different advisory groups or classes race each other to run to a spot, grab a tie, successfully tie it, get approval from a parent or judge, then return to tag the next person. Be sure that the advisors participate too! Parents will be thrilled you have found a fun way to teach this skill.

- Have a vertical mentoring program in your school or district where older students work with younger students on a regular basis, participating in fun activities, sharing community service, and attending athletic events together. The older students can also read stories and observe as the younger students do classroom presentations. Parents can help support this program by driving their older (or younger) student to the location for mentoring.

- Involve parents with their children in a campus clean-up or landscaping events. Be sure that teachers and principals attend too! This can bond all constituents for a fun afternoon.

- Host a "Bike and Walk to School Day" for your students and parents. Choose a location for bikers and a separate location for walkers to meet fifteen minutes from the school. Have students, parents, and interested teachers bike or walk to school as a group. Prior to the event teach children about safety for walking or biking to school. Ask local police to be present during the event—it's always nice when kids can see police officers in a positive role.

WRAPPING UP THE MAIN POINTS

Developing strong relationships with both boys and girls promotes motivation and performance, especially as you

- Use both verbal and nonverbal communication to reach students with differentiated ways of "hearing"

- Help girls learn to manage emotions so that they can be stronger and less distracted by drama, especially during adolescence

- Develop trusting relationships with boys so that they are more willing to be vulnerable and share feelings that they often keep buried

- Provide discipline in gender-friendly ways

- Help your boys and girls connect with same-sex mentors

EPILOGUE

No two students start the race to be educated with the same amount of preparation, but it is our responsibility as educators to meet them where they are. We must give rollerblades to some, skateboards to others, or even bikes. As educators we must differentiate for each individual's needs. We must build confidence and relentlessly pursue academic gains to ensure that even if our students start the race late they will finish.

—Anastasia Michals, 6th grade math teacher

Teaching boys and girls can indeed feel like a race—it moves fast, there are lots of high expectations, and some kids fall behind. Everyone on the sidelines hopes for the best outcomes for everyone, and because we all love children, we each feel called in our own way to try to help every racer succeed.

As we work with schools across America and around the world, we listen to the stories of teachers and students. Though the places, the teachers, and the kids vary greatly, the stories are often very similar. We find both boys and girls—not all of them, certainly, but far too many—who are disconnected, disengaged, disinterested, and underperforming. For many of them, "school" does not engage their spirits, does not help them become the learners they were born to be, and does not help them finish the race.

As you and your schools and communities work to find ways to help children become engaged, successful learners, we hope you'll consider single-sex options. Single-sex classes can honor and address the core nature and hardwired biology of our boys and girls.

We hope the knowledge that so many practitioners have shared in this book will provide you with new tools and skills. Our mission in all our own work as trainers and researchers is to help professionals merge the science of learning differences with the intuitive art of classroom practice. You are scientists and you are artists. Both the science and the art need support, research, understanding, and inspiration.

We hope you have found this book helpful, and we hope you will contact us with your success stories and your innovations. One classroom and one community at a time, you have the power to change the future for every child.

SOURCES

PART ONE

Povich, Elaine S. "Clinton for Same Sex Schools." *Newsday,* May 10, 2002. Available from www.Newsday.com.

U.S. Department of Education. "Secretary Spellings Announces More Choices in Single Sex Education." *ED.gov.* Available from www.ed.gov/news/pressreleases/2006/10/10242006 .html.

Chapter One

Baron-Cohen, Simon. (2003). *The Essential Difference: The Truth About the Male and Female Brain.* New York: Basic Books.

Blum, Deborah. (1998). *Sex on the Brain: The Biological Differences Between Men and Women.* New York: Penguin Books.

Carter, Rita. (1998). *Mapping the Mind.* Berkeley: University of California Press.

Jensen, Eric. (2000). *Brain-Based Learning: The New Science of Teaching and Learning.* (Rev. ed.) San Diego, Calif.: Brain Store.

Jensen, Eric. (2006). *Enriching the Brain: How to Maximize Every Learner's Potential.* San Francisco: Jossey-Bass.

Moir, Anne, and Jessel, David. (1992). *Brain Sex: The Real Difference Between Men and Women.* New York: Delta.

Rhoads, Steven E. (2004). *Taking Sex Differences Seriously.* San Francisco: Encounter Books.

Salomone, Rosemary C. (2003). *Same, Different, Equal: Rethinking Single-Sex Schooling.* New Haven, Conn.: Yale University Press.

Sax, Leonard. (2005). *Why Gender Matters.* New York: Broadway Books. See also www.singlesexschools.org.

Sousa, David A. (2001). *How the Brain Learns.* (2nd ed.) Thousand Oaks, Calif.: Corwin Press.

Stabiner, Karen. "Boys Here, Girls There: Sure, If Equality's the Goal." *Washington Post,* May 12, 2002. Available from www.washingtonpost.com.

U.S. Department of Education. Document 34 CFR Part 106, the complete Title IX regulations, is available and may be downloaded directly from the Department of Education Web site: www.ed.gov/index.jhtml.

Wolfe, Patricia. (2001). *Brain Matters: Translating Research into Classroom Practice.* Alexandria, Va.: Association for Supervision and Curriculum Development.

Chapter Two

Brizendine, Louann. (2006). *The Female Brain.* New York: Broadway Books.

Conlin, Michelle. "The New Gender Gap." *Business Week,* May 26, 2003. Retrieved Mar. 20, 2007, from www.businessweek.com.

Gurian, Michael, and Stevens, Kathy. "With Boys and Girls in Mind." *Educational Leadership,* Nov. 2004, *62*(3), pp. 21–26.

Gurian, Michael, and Stevens, Kathy. (2005). *The Minds of Boys.* San Francisco: Jossey-Bass.

Indiana University. "Men Do Hear—But Differently Than Women, Brain Images Show." *Science Daily,* Nov. 29, 2000. Retrieved Apr. 27, 2008, from www.sciencedaily.com /releases/2000/11/ 001129075326.htm.

Motivation & Engagement in School. Retrieved Apr. 27, 2008, from Boys and Schools—A Project of Men's Health Network: www.boysandschools.com.

Salomone, Rosemary. "Putting Single-Sex Schooling Back on Course." *Education Week,* Dec. 6, 2006, *26*(14), pp. 32–33, 43.

Shaywitz, Bennett A., and Shaywitz, Sally E. "Sex Differences in the Functional Organization of the Brain for Language." *Nature,* Feb. 16, 1995, *373,* pp. 607–609. Retrieved Apr. 30, 2008, from www.nature.com.

Sousa, David A. (2006). *How the Brain Learns.* Thousand Oaks, Calif.: Corwin Press.

PART TWO
Chapter Three

National Association of State Boards of Education. NASBE Policy Update, Vol. 10, No. 11. Available from Department of Education, Mary E. Switzer Building, 330 C Street S.W., Room 5036, Washington, D.C.

Ravitch, Diane. "Why Not a Girls School?" *New York Post,* Sept. 26, 1997.

Spielhagen, Frances. (2007). *Debating Single-Sex Education: Separate and Equal?* Lanham, Md.: Rowman & Littlefield.

Spielhagen, Frances. *P.A.S.-S.A.© Parents Assess Single-Sex Arrangements.* Used with permission.

PART THREE

Wright, Benjamin. (2008). *Yes We Can If We Choose.* Danvers, Mass.: American Books.

Chapter Five

Cohen, Isabel, and Goldsmith, Marcelle. (2002/2003). *Hands On: How to Use Brain Gym®
in the Classroom.* Ventura, Calif.: Edu-Kinesthetics.

Dennison, Paul E., and Dennison, Gail E. (1989). *Brain Gym®.* Ventura, Calif.: Edu-Kinesthetics.

Jensen, Eric. (2000). *Learning with the Body in Mind: The Scientific Basis for Energizers,
Movement, Play, Games, and Physical Education.* San Diego, Calif.: Brain Store.

Montgomery, Rick. "Hard-Wired to Learn?" *Kansas City Star,* December 5, 2005.

Promislow, Sharon. (2005). *Making the Brain/Body Connection—A Playful Guide to
Releasing Mental, Physical, and Emotional Blocks to Success.* Vancouver, Canada:
Enhanced Learning & Integration.

Pytel, Barbara. "Temperature and Learning: How Hot and Cold Affect the Brain." *Educational Issues,* Aug. 7, 2006. Available from http://educationalissues.suite101.com/
article.cfm/temperature_and_learning.

Sax, Leonard. (2007). *Boys Adrift.* New York: Basic Books.

Chapter Six

Adolescent Brain Development: Vulnerabilities and Opportunities. *New York Academy of
Science Annual,* June 2004, *1021,* pp. 143–147.

Clay, Daniel, Vignoles, Vivian, and Dittma, Helga. "Body Image and Self-Esteem Among
Adolescent Girls: Testing the Influence of Sociocultural Factors." *Journal of Research
on Adolescence,* 2005, *15*(4), pp. 451–477.

Deak, JoAnn, with Barker, Teresa. (2002) *Girls Will Be Girls: Raising Confident and Courageous Daughters.* New York: Hyperion Books.

Hinduja, Sameer, and Patchin, Justin W. (2009). *Bullying Beyond the Schoolyard: Preventing, and Responding to Cyberbullying.* Thousand Oaks, Calif.: Corwin Press.

Mlambo-Ngcuka, Phumzile. *Addresses and Speeches by Deputy President of South Africa,
Ms. Phumzile.* Retrieved June 15, 2008, from www.dfa.gov.za/docs/speeches/mlambo_
ngcuka.htm.

National Association of School Psychologists. "Girls Bullying Girls: An Introduction to
Relational Aggression." May 21, 2008. Retrieved from www.teachersandfamilies.com/
open/parent/ra1.cfm.

"Shortchanging Girls, Shortchanging America." American Association of University
Women, 1991. Executive summary. Retrieved Aug. 28, 2008, from www.aauw.org/
research/sgsa.cfm.

Simmons, Rachel. (2002). *Odd Girl Out: The Hidden Culture of Aggression in Girls.* New York: Harcourt.

Willis, Judy. "Cooperative Learning Is a Brain Turn On." *Middle School Journal,* Mar. 2007, *38*(4).

Wiseman, Rosalind. (2002). *Queen Bees & Wannabes: Helping Your Daughter Survive Cliques, Gossip, Boyfriends, and Other Realities of Adolescence.* New York: Three Rivers Press.

Chapter Seven

Amen, Daniel. (2005). *Making a Good Brain Great: The Amen Clinic Program for Achieving and Sustaining Optimal Mental Performance.* New York: Harmony Books.

Celebrating Multiple Intelligences: Teaching for Success—A Practical Guide Created by the Faculty of The New City School. (1997). St. Louis, Mo.: The New City School.

Fletcher, Ralph. (2006). *Boy Writers—Reclaiming Their Voices.* Portland, Me.: Stenhouse.

Gurian, Michael, and Trueman, Terry. (2000). *What Stories Does My Son Need?: A Guide to Books and Movies That Build Character in Boys.* Los Angeles: Tarcher.

Jensen, Eric. (2003). *Tools for Engagement: Managing Emotional States for Learner Success.* San Diego, Calif.: Brain Store.

Jung, Carl. Retrieved from www.quotegarden.com/teacher-apprec.html.

Knowles, Elizabeth, and Smith, Martha. (2005). *Boys and Literacy: Practical Strategies for Librarians, Teachers, and Parents.* Westport, Conn.: Libraries Unlimited.

Me Read? No Way! A Practical Guide to Improving Boys' Literacy Skills. (2004). Ontario, Canada, Ministry of Education. Available from www.edu.gov.on.ca.

Moloney, James. (2002). "Ideas for Getting Boys to Read." Available from www.home.gil.com.au/~cbcqld/moloney/books7.htm.

Odean, Kathleen. (1997). *Great Books for Boys: More Than 600 Books for Boys, 2 to 14.* New York: Ballantine.

Papert, Seymour. "Project-Based Learning." Retrieved Sept. 5, 2008, from www.edutopia.org/seymour-papert-project-based-learning.

Scieszka, Jon. *Guys Read.* Available from www.guysread.com.

Sullivan, Michael. *Books for Boys.* Available from www.geocities.com/talestoldtall/BooksforBoys.html.

Taylor, Donna L. "Not Just Boring Stories: Reconsidering the Gender Gap for Boys." *Journal of Adolescent & Adult Literacy,* Jan. 2005, *48*(4).

Wilson, Gary. (2003). "Using the National Healthy School Standard to Raise Boys' Achievement." Department for Education and Skills, UK. Available from www.standards.dfes.gov.uk/genderandachievement/.

Chapter Eight

Christie, Alice A. "How Adolescent Boys and Girls View Today's Computer Culture." Report to the United States Congress, 2002, by the National Science Foundation. Retrieved Nov. 27, 2006, from www.education-world.com/a_curr/profdev026.shtml.

Cooper-Mullin, Alison, and Coye, Jennifer. (1998). *Once Upon a Heroine: 400 Books for Girls to Love.* Chicago: Contemporary Books.

Delisio, Ellen R. (2002). *Sheila Tobias on Rethinking Teaching Math, Science.* Education World. www.education-world.com/a_curr/profdev026.shtml.

Dodson, Shireen. (1998). *100 Books for Girls to Grow On.* New York: Harper-Collins.

National Coalition of Girls' Schools. Information available from www.ncgs.org.

New City School. *Celebrating Multiple Intelligences: Teaching for Success—A Practical Guide Created by the Faculty of The New City School.* (1997). St. Louis, Mo.: The New City School.

Odean, Kathleen. (1998). *Great Books for Girls.* New York: Ballantine.

Sprague, Marsha, and Keating, Kara. (2007). *Discovering Their Voices.* Newark, Del.: International Reading Association.

Teenreads.com. Available at www.teenreads.com.

Williams, Bronwyn T. "Girl Power in a Digital World: Considering the Complexity of Gender, Literacy, and Technology." *Journal of Adolescent & Adult Literacy*, 2006, *50*, pp. 300–306.

Wycoff, Joyce. (1991). *Mindmapping: Your Personal Guide to Exploring Creativity and Problem-Solving.* New York: Penguin Putnam.

Chapter Nine

Claytionary. Information available from www.kieve.org/leadership/followup/claytionary.pdf.

Joseph, Gail E., and Strain, Phillip S. (2002). *Enhancing Emotional Vocabulary in Young Children.* The Center on the Social and Emotional Foundations for Early Learning, www.csefel.uluc.edu. Champaign: University of Illinois at Urbana-Champaign.

Slocumb, Paul D. (2004). *Hear Our Cry.* Highlands, Tex.: aha! Process.

INDEX

Dodson, S., 210
Dopamine, 30–31
Double Hands Math Game, 194
Douglas, J., 200
Drama, 228
Drawing, 170, 238, 241

E

Edmunds, S., 176
Edwards, B. R., 181–182
Elementary schools: single-sex program creation in, 51; success stories of, 9–10
Emotions: benefits of single-sex classrooms and, 38; brain structure and, 26–27; in girl-friendly classrooms, 123, 134; helping boys with, 236–241
Empathy, 132, 247
Encouragement, 124, 140
Energy Yawns, 99–100
Enhancing Emotional Vocabulary in Young Children (Joseph & Strain), 238
Estrogen, 30
Evening lectures, 247
Exercise. *See* Physical activity

F

Facial expressions, 134
Fantasy Vacation activity, 196–197
Fatherless children, 234
Female scientists, 208
"Fight or flight" response, 26
Flesch-Kincaid Readability scale, 74
Fletcher, R., 171–172
Florida schools, 9–10, 16
Florida Writes test, 16
Football games, 155–156
Fowler, C., 93, 157, 193, 196–197
Frontal cortex, 25
Furniture, 89, 94–95, 104–105

G

Game-oriented activities, 110, 154–57, 194–197
Gender equality, as mission of single-sex classrooms, 4
Gender gap: current state of, 32; effects of, 32–35; in language arts achievement, 167; parents' concerns about, 67
Generalizations, making, 31
Girl Scouts, 231
Girl-friendly classrooms: addressing body image in, 129–130; basic strategies for, 119–120; benefits of, 119; bullying in, 126–129, 130; classroom environment in, 120–121; collaboration in, 133–138; competition in, 138–139, 196; emotions in, 123; examples of, 115–118; handling stress in, 124–125; increasing self-esteem in, 123–124; language arts strategies in, 209–216; leadership in, 131–133; mathematics strategies in, 188–199; relational aggression and, 126–129, 130; risk taking in, 119; sample activities for, 130–131; science strategies in, 199–204; social studies strategies in, 217–219; successful teachers in, 139–142; technology strategies in, 204–208
Girls: achievement gap of, 35–38; benefits of single-sex instruction for, 6–7, 38–40; versus boys, in science class, 199–200; brain chemistry of, 29–31; brain processing of, 27–29; brain structure of, 23–27; challenges of, 121; code of behavior for, 122–123; definition of technology from, 205; forming relationships with, 225–232, 244–249; generalizations about, 31; in single-sex classrooms, success stories of, 7–13; stereotypes

Neurotransmitters: definition of, 21–22; types of, 30–31
Nevada schools, 55
New York schools, 16–17
Nina B. Hollis Institute for Educational Reform, 38
North Carolina schools, 12–13, 94–95, 179, 181
Nutrition, 130–131, 248

O

Obesity, 129–130
Odd Girl Speaks (Simmons), 130
Odean, K., 163, 210, 211
Oklahoma schools, 10
Once Upon a Heroine: 400 Books for Girls to Love (Cooper-Mullin & Coye), 211
100 Black Men of Atlanta, 7
100 Books for Girls to Grow On (Dodson), 210
Optimism, 53
Opt-in programs, 9–10
Organization, classroom, 104
Outdoor classrooms, 107
Oxytocin, 31

P

Pair-share activities, 95
Paper pickup, 101
Papert, S., 158
Parent surveys: for program creation, 69–70; for program evaluation, 74, 80–81
Parents: boy-friendly classrooms and, 87; building relationships with, 248–250; in program evaluation, 74, 80–81; in single-sex program creation, 48, 65–70
Parker, R., 11
Participation, classroom, 6
Patchin, J. W., 127, 129

Pattern activities, 101
Peisner, J., 246
Physical activity: in boy-friendly classrooms, 93–102, 148–149; brain structure and, 25; gender gap and, 33; in girl-friendly classrooms, 130; importance of, 94
Physical education classes, 96–97
Physical science, 202
Poetry, 173–178
Pollack, W. S., 32
Positron emission tomography (PET), 23
Post, T., 183–185
Principals, 50–51, 53
Problem solving, 119, 124, 153
Project-based learning, 158–160, 208
Promethean Boards, 8
Promislow, S., 98
Prompts, writing, 214–215
Pyeatt, S., 134, 135, 149, 247

Q

Queen Bees and Wannabes (Wiseman), 130
Questioning, 140–141

R

Ramp Up to Advanced Literacy program, 166
Rap activities, 198, 213
Ravitch, D., 45
Reading. *See* Literacy
Reading groups, 212
Reading levels, 74
Recess, 88, 96–97
Recruiting students, 47
Reflection, 147–148, 178
Relational aggression, 37, 126–129, 130
Relationships: with boys, forming, 232–248; brain chemistry and, 31;

STRATEGIES FOR TEACHING BOYS AND GIRLS
Elementary Level
A Workbook for Educators

By: Michael Gurian, Kathy Stevens, and Kelley King

ISBN: 978-0-7879-9730-4 | Paperback

"The authors have created a vital resource for teachers and administrators who are striving to conquer the gender gap in their schools."
—Dr. Joseph M. Porto, superintendent, Avoca School District 37, Wilmette, IL

The **Strategies for Teaching Boys and Girls** books offer teachers a hands-on resource that draws on the Gurian Institute's research and training with schools and school districts. The workbooks present practical strategies, lessons, and activities that have been field-tested in real classrooms and developed to harness boys' and girls' unique strengths.

STRATEGIES FOR TEACHING BOYS AND GIRLS
Secondary Level
A Workbook for Educators

By: Michael Gurian, Kathy Stevens, and Kelley King

ISBN: 978-0-7879-9731-1 | Paperback

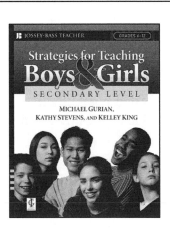

"The Gurian Institute provides us with powerful research put in practical form that will do amazing things in our classrooms and in our students' lives."
—Renee Parker, assistant principal (9th and 10th grades), Hope High School, Hope, AR

THE MINDS OF BOYS
Saving Our Sons from Falling Behind in School and Life

By: Michael Gurian and Kathy Stevens

ISBN: 978-0-7879-9528-7 | Paperback

"Michael Gurian and Kathy Stevens pull the pieces together in The Minds of Boys, *including the social, emotional, physical, and cognitive needs of boys. This is a must-read for educators from preschool through young adulthood and for any parent or grandparent who is raising a boy. This book is well researched, offering concrete ways to help our boys develop and flourish in and out of school."*
—Dr. Paul D. Slocumb, author, *Hear Our Cry: Boys in Crisis*

*"*The Minds of Boys *is an excellent read. I found it enlightening not only as a neuroscientist but also as the mother of a young boy. It has absolutely changed the way that I think about boys (and men) and the ways in which they express their enthusiasm for life."*
—Tracey J. Shors, Ph.D., Department of Psychology, Center for Collaborative Neuroscience, Rutgers University

In ***The Minds of Boys***, Gurian shows parents and teachers how to help boys overcome their current classroom obstacles by helping to create the proper learning environment, understand how to help boys work with their unique natural gifts, nurture and expand every bit of their potential, and enable them to succeed in life.

Gurian presents a whole new way of solving the "boy's crisis" based on the success of his program in schools across the country, the latest research and application of neuro-biological research on how boys' brains actually work and how they can learn very well when they're properly taught.

Anyone who cares about the future of our boys must read this book.

BOYS AND GIRLS LEARN DIFFERENTLY!
A Guide for Teachers and Parents

By: Michael Gurian

ISBN: 978-0-7879-6117-6 | Paperback

"The insights and innovations in Boys and Girls Learn Differently! *have been applied in our classrooms with phenomenal success, leading to better academic performance and better behavior. I highly recommend this book to all parents, teachers, and school administrators."*

—Dan Colgan, superintendent of schools, St. Joseph, Missouri

"Boys and Girls Learn Differently! offers valuable and much-needed tools to provide boys and girls with true equal educational opportunities. The new techniques Michael Gurian presents here will transform our classrooms and the way parents teach their children in very positive ways."

—John Gray, author, *Children Are from Heaven* and *Men Are from Mars, Women Are from Venus*

In this profoundly significant book, author Michael Gurian synthesizes the current scientific evidence and clearly demonstrates how the distinction in hard-wiring and socialized gender differences affects how boys and girls learn. Gurian presents a new way to educate our children based on brain science, neurological development, and chemical and hormonal disparities. The innovations presented in this book were applied in the classroom and proven successful, with dramatic improvements in test scores, during a two-year study that Gurian and his colleagues conducted in six Missouri school districts.

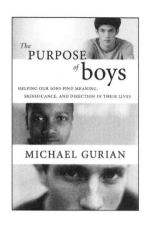

THE PURPOSE OF BOYS

Helping Our Sons Find Meaning, Significance, and Direction in Their Lives

By: Michael Gurian

ISBN: 978-0-470-24337-4 | Hardcover

AVAILABLE APRIL 2009

A CRUCIAL BOOK IN THE GROUNDBREAKING SERIES ON BOYS AND FOLLOW-UP TO THE BEST-SELLING *THE MINDS OF BOYS*

*"**There is no one who understands the development of boys better than Michael Gurian.** In this insightful new book, Gurian offers useful advice about how to help boys succeed in the key challenge of today's world, finding purpose in life. Parents and others who care about the future of young people will benefit greatly from this book."*

—William Damon, Professor of Education, Stanford University; author, *The Path to Purpose: Helping our Children find their Calling in Life*

"The Purpose of Boys provides a clear, research-based view on the significance of fully committing ourselves to the important task of raising our sons. It gives us a useful, applicable set of tools and strategies to do so."

—Harold S. Koplewicz, M.D., Founder and Director, NYU Child Study Center

In this climax to his series of landmark boys books which includes *The Wonder of Boys* and *The Minds of Boys*, Michael Gurian offers a powerful new program for creating core purpose in our sons by building morality, character, career goals, the ability to form intimate relationships, selflessness, personal and community responsibility, and an accelerated process of developmental maturity.

Gurian draws on the latest science and field research on how boys develop neurologically and the unique issues they must confront. He guides parents and educators to customize their support and interventions according to the unique needs, weaknesses, and strengths of each individual boy and young man.